The
LEGACY
of
ATLANTIS

The

LEGACY

of

ATLANTIS

GORDON DONNELL

THE LEGACY OF ATLANTIS

iUniverse books may be ordered through booksellers or by contacting:

iUniverse
1663 Liberty Drive
Bloomington, IN 47403
www.iuniverse.com
844-349-9409

ISBN: 978-1-6632-1383-9 (sc)
ISBN: 978-1-6632-1384-6 (e)

Print information available on the last page.

iUniverse rev. date: 11/19/2020

DEDICATION

This work is dedicated to the explorers, excavators, technicians and translators who have devoted their lives to finding, extracting and making sense of the surviving fragments of human activity in the distant past. Their stories and struggles are seldom recounted, but without their efforts and achievements neither this nor any other book of ancient history could be written.

INTRODUCTION

The legend of the lost continent of Atlantis has captured the collective imagination as few other tales have done. A utopian civilization fallen from grace. A great land mass riven by earthquakes and sinking beneath the waves. An empire vanishing into the mists of time.

Books on Atlantis have been written by the thousands. Explorers have scoured the world to find the undersea remains of the continent. Psychics have held séances to contact the departed souls of its inhabitants. Even comic books have gotten into the act. In one the Atlanteans were found alive and well in their sunken capitol, breathing through gills and dancing the bop while a jukebox plugged into an electric eel howled jive.

Beneath the veneer of fantasy and foolishness lies a core of fact. In the last century archaeologists began connecting the dots between the legend and the physical evidence they were uncovering. There had once been an Atlantis, although we do not know what the inhabitants called it. And it was destroyed in a cataclysm.

The legend that has come down to us is not without exaggeration. Atlantis was neither a continent nor was it ever entirely submerged. We will begin by examining the origin of the story of Atlantis. Then we will visit the remains of the site and learn something of the civilization that built and populated it.

While we are there we will examine the mechanics of the destruction wrought by nature. We will also gain an appreciation of its power. Involved was a release of energy exceeding that which would be produced by the simultaneous detonation of the world's entire nuclear and thermo-nuclear arsenals.

That energy release, and its interaction with the world's geography and weather, had a global impact on the civilizations of the time. Not all were literate, but some contemporary writing has survived. In addition, lore has made its way into later literature and written history. We will examine these sources for clues to what befell the people caught in the aftermath of the destruction.

Physical evidence continues to be unearthed by archaeologists. Previous discoveries have been re-analyzed in light of new information, using increasingly sophisticated techniques and technology. DNA mapping has given us a more detailed picture of the ancient world and its people.

The wealth of emerging evidence brings its own issues. It comes to us in fragments that must be pieced together to construct a comprehensible narrative. Not all of the evidence tells the same story. Some does not conform to currently accepted views of timing and events from the period.

We will examine the evidence in the context of the underlying science to identify and attempt to resolve the contradictions. Some of what we will discover will clarify our understanding of long known events and interactions. Some of it will demand a rethinking of current beliefs.

The destruction of Atlantis is a fact of history. The aftermath of that destruction re-shaped civilization and left a legacy we are just now on the threshold of understanding.

THE LEGEND OF ATLANTIS

The popular version of the legend of Atlantis is that the story comes from the writings of the Greek philosopher Plato. This is true only to a point. Plato unfolds the tale of Atlantis in two of his works, titled *Timeaus* and *Critias*. He is careful to tell the reader that his narrative is sourced from the Egyptian priesthood. Specifically, the story was told to Solon on a journey he made to the Egyptian city of Sais in the Nile delta. Solon later entrusted the information to an ancestor of Critias named Dropides. The tale was passed down the family line to Critias.

Solon was an actual person, a widely travelled Athenian aristocrat, poet and member of the city's government. The best approximation we have of his lifetime is that he was born in 638 BC and died in 558 BC. Plato was also an Athenian aristocrat, as well as a member of one of the city's wealthiest families. There is some debate as to whether he was born in 428 BC or 424 BC. He died in 348 BC.

At this point a note on dates is in order. It has become fashionable to substitute the abbreviations BCE (Before Common Era) and CE (Common Era) for the traditional BC (Before Christ) and AD (Anno Domini – in the year of our lord). Regardless of terminology, the system of dating is based on work completed by a monk named Dionysius Exiguus around 525 AD. Years are numbered from a fixed year attributed by his research to the birth of Christ. The system came into common usage after 731 AD, when the

Venerable Bede applied it in his *Ecclesiastical History of the English People.* We will use the traditional nomenclature, not for any religious purpose but to retain a sense of how dates are arrived at. Since date derivation will loom large in later chapters the floating nomenclatures BP (Before Present) and ya (years ago) are also avoided.

The exact dates of Plato's writings are currently debated. The dramatic date of the dialogues dealing with Atlantis appears to be around 425 BC. The general time frame makes Plato's version of the passage of the tale of Atlantis from Solon through Dropides to Critias chronologically possible. Plato also points out that since the tale was told in Egyptian, the reader is at the mercy of Solon's translation into Greek. According to Plato the translation was undertaken so that Solon could use the story in his own poems. The writings of Solon exist today only as fragments of a much larger whole. The surviving fragments contain no mention of Atlantis.

Plato's title characters, Timaeus of Locris and Critias, are not directly traceable to actual people. Locris is a city in Southern Italy, of which little is known. Folk wisdom defines an expert as anyone who is more than fifty miles from home. Timaeus appears to be an invention, perhaps inspired by someone Plato knew or knew of, but essentially created to fill the role of a learned soul bringing wisdom from afar; a savant who could expound believably on the physical properties of the universe and the nature of humankind. He is not a direct source of information on Atlantis.

Athens had more than one notable named Critias around Plato's time. One of the candidates is Plato's maternal great grandfather, one of the Thirty Tyrants, a group of oligarchs who controlled Athens briefly in the aftermath of the Peloponnesian War. Scholars have nominated other favorites. None of the candidates has been established. There is no evidence that Critias was more than a convenient name for a cast member in the drama; an aristocrat who might conceivably have fallen heir to the story of Atlantis. It would be unusual, however, that Plato would have selected a name notable among Athenians if he did not have a real person in mind.

Plato's writings on the subject of Atlantis, *Timaeus* and *Critias,* are in the form of dialogues. The reader is made to feel that he is present at conversations the two title characters had with Plato's predecessor and mentor, the well known philosopher Socrates. Socrates was born in 470 BC and was executed in 399 BC. He would have been about forty five years of age at the time of the conversations. Socrates was unique among philosophers in that he left no writings of his own. He is known only through the writings of Plato and other followers. The dialogues predate his acquaintance with Plato, and perhaps even Plato's birth.

Timaeus is a completed and carefully crafted work. The title character expounds at length on Plato's view of the world. It seems unlikely that Plato would associate either his ideas or those of his mentor, Socrates, with the tale of Atlantis unless he believed the core story to be both historical fact and support for his philosophy.

Critias ends abruptly. It was apparently unfinished at Plato's death. This should not be taken to mean that Plato was in the process of writing the dialogue when he passed away. *Critias* was not a draft. It was an edited piece that had been either abandoned or put aside with the intent of finishing it later. Plato's entire body of writing is believed to have survived intact. No subsequent work on *Critias* is known to exist.

The first mention of Atlantis occurs at the beginning of *Timaeus*. Socrates has given a philosophical discourse on the characteristics of the ideal society. He is worried that his presentation lacks any foundation in the real world. Timaeus tells Socrates that Critias, who is also present in this dialogue, knows of an actual ideal society that once existed at a long forgotten time in Athens. Critias provides little description of Atlantis in *Timaeus*. He is content to vilify its rulers to emphasize the virtue of the ancient Athenian society. He will provide a detailed account of Atlantis and its civilization in his own dialogue, although his brief recitation in *Timaeus* stands on its own merit rather than merely serving as a preview of coming attractions.

According to Critias, Atlantis was an island larger than Libya and Asia located beyond the Pillars of Hercules. The Pillars of Hercules are thought to refer to the Strait of Gibraltar, the gateway from the Mediterranean Sea to the Atlantic Ocean. At the time Libya was a reference to all of non-Egyptian Africa. Fitting a land mass the size of those two continents into the Atlantic Ocean would have been a geographic impossibility. A worldwide displacement of sea water would have been involved. The statement calls into question Plato's knowledge of the world.

Critias tells Socrates that the rulers of Atlantis conquered and enslaved many of the lands bordering the Mediterranean. They were preparing to move against Egypt and Greece. 9,000 years before the time of Solon, the citizens of Athens defeated the Atlanteans in battle, saved themselves and Egypt and reversed Atlantis' previous conquests.

At a later time both Athens and Atlantis were destroyed in a day and a night by earthquakes and floods of extraordinary violence. All records of the old Athens were lost. Atlantis sank into the sea. The sinking, we are told by Plato, resulted in an accumulation of mud that rendered the sea beyond the Pillars of Hercules, the Atlantic Ocean, too shallow for navigation. Where this bit of nonsense came from is anyone's guess.

Plato's assertion that Atlantis was destroyed 9,000 years before the time of Solon is also open to question. Solon's source is Egyptian. The Egyptians did not reckon the passage of years from a fixed date. Instead they reset their calendar each time a new Pharaoh ascended to the throne. Had Solon been given a year for the destruction of Atlantis, it likely would have been the regnal year of the Pharaoh in power when the destruction took place. Reference to a sitting Pharaoh may in fact exist in Egyptian records pertaining to Atlantis' destruction. We will examine that possibility in a later chapter.

Critias' statement that the sum of years elapsed between the destruction of Atlantis and the time of Solon was 9,000 has become a centerpiece of arguments that the legend of Atlantis was pure invention. An elapsed time of 9,000 years would put the conflict between Athens and Atlantis in the Stone Age, long before the rise of any known cities or nations.

The situation is not as straightforward as it may seem. The critics' arguments are based on currently available copies of Plato's works. The ancients had difficulty expressing the concept of zero. For example, the Babylonians, whom we will meet later, wrote the numbers 12, 102 and 1200 in exactly the same way. The reader was left to intuit the meaning from context. We do not have Plato's original manuscript so we do not know how he wrote the number 9,000. He may have done his best to write 900, and left us at the mercy of the interpretations of later copyists. A date 900 years before the time of Solon would place the Atlantean cataclysm in the Bronze Age of Mycenaean Greece, an era for which Plato had no record beyond poems and stories, but during which cities, nations and empires flourished.

A more likely example of invention by Plato is the Egyptian priests' mention of the myth of Deucalion. Deucalion is the Greek version of the Biblical flood story. There is also a version of the story in the Sumerian *Epic of Gilgamesh*, but no mention of a singular flood exists in known Egyptian writing.

Critics also point to the motives and character of Plato. He was active in arguing against the naval expansion by Athens taking place during his lifetime. He was a philosopher and not a historian; a man more likely to be interested in parable than in fact.

Taken alone the brief account of the destruction of Atlantis at the beginning of *Timaeus* may seem less than credible. When viewed in context, a different conclusion emerges. *Timaeus* was not primarily a philosophical discourse. It was Plato's attempt to describe the physical laws governing the universe and the rules applicable to the human condition. The topics covered by the title character span the range of Greek knowledge and thinking in Plato's time. They include astronomy, anatomy, geometry, medicine, chemistry and physics. Plato's intent was to produce a factual treatise.

Every author, Plato included, writes with an audience in mind. In Plato's case it was the Athenians of his time. To gain support for his ideas, he had to couch his rhetoric in terms they identified with, even at the expense of some factual imprecision. This is common throughout the history of writing. As an example from today, writers do not hesitate to use King Kong and Godzilla as metaphors for bestial destruction, even though no modern city has ever been terrorized by a giant ape or demolished by a radioactive dinosaur.

The detailed descriptions of Atlantis and Atlantean civilization come to us from Plato's *Critias*. In this work the title character supports the accuracy of his narrative by expanding on his claim that he is referencing information given by Solon to his ancestor, Dropides. He also claims to have studied Solon's manuscript of translation from Egyptian references to Greek equivalents. Critias' presentation is entirely verbal. He never displays any of the documents to his audience, Socrates. Plato's Athenian audience wanted the story in Athenian, not Egyptian, terms. Plato used the claims of Critias to comply.

According to Critias Atlantis was created by the Greek God Posiedon to house his human consort Cleito and their five sets of twin offspring. Citing the accomplishments of a Greek God would have been heresy for the Egyptian priesthood. By citing an Egyptian source for the tale of Atlantis, Plato has painted himself into a corner. He can preserve Critias' credibility only by warning the reader not to be surprised by cultural anomalies because Solon has translated Egyptian references into Greek equivalents, and further by asserting that Solon's translation documents have been studied by Critias. It seems unlikely that a writer of Plato's skill and experience would create this level of difficulty for himself and potential confusion for his reader unless he knew or believed Egypt to be the true source of the story of Atlantis.

Critias tells Socrates that Posiedon fortified the hill where Cleito lived by surrounding it with three rings of sea and two of land, like cartwheels on a concentric hub, set at specific proportional distances one from the other. Since there were no ships in that early time of history, Cleito's sanctuary was inaccessible to man. Proportionality was an important element of Greek thinking in Plato's time, and may have influenced his description of Atlantis.

Posiedon subdivided Atlantis among his offspring. The eldest was designated to rule over the others, who maintained subordinate fiefdoms. Generations passed, the population grew and Atlantis developed an economic infrastructure and maritime technology. Critias provides a detailed physical description of the subdivision and development of Atlantis, including precise measurements of the components. Such a description might have had its roots in Egypt. Annual flooding of the Nile forced the Egyptians to regularly re-establish boundaries of farms bordering the river. They were skilled surveyors and keenly aware of land measurement. In addition, Plato mentions the presence of elephants in Atlantis, not something a Greek philosopher would think to invent.

According to Critias, the land mass at the center of Atlantis' three rings of water was the original home of Cleito, a hill of no great height. After fortifying it, Posiedon created two springs, one producing cold water, and the other hot. In time the area came to hold a palace, temples, a protective military garrison and a horse racing track. This was enclosed by walls constructed from stone of various colors quarried on Atlantis. The surrounding rings of land were connected by communicating bridges a hundred feet wide and guarded against intrusion. This suggests an advanced, self-indulgent and hierarchical society easily recognizable by the Athenians.

The outlying lands of Atlantis were organized into symmetrical agricultural plots. Graze was set aside for animal husbandry. Mineral resources and timber were abundant. A great amount of labor was lavished on a large and complex harbor. The harbor wall was built closely around with houses and the harbor was constantly full of shipping from all locations. Entry was through a canal wide enough to pass triremes and then through a series of locks.

The reference to triremes is an anachronism. The trireme was an ancient naval assault vessel with three banks of oars to bring it to ramming speed during conflict. Based on examples from the later Roman Punic Wars, the ram was a multi-pronged bronze projection securely attached to the forward edge of the keel below the waterline. It required considerable force to penetrate the hull of an opposing ship. The impact would have generated a corresponding counter shock to the attacking vessel. This arrangement became practical only after ship builders began using a keel and framing for the structural members of their vessels. Prior to that, boats were built with the outer hull as the main structural member. They likely could not have withstood the impact of ramming. Triremes did not come into common use until the Seventh Century BC.

There are also technical details in Plato's description that seem out of place. For example, the buildings of Atlantis are described as having gleaming decorative facades and interiors that included an unknown precious metal called orichalcum. What orichalcum was and why it was mentioned in describing buildings that were otherwise little different from opulent structures to be seen in Plato's time remains a mystery. These and other anomalies raise the possibility that the narrative contained in *Critias* is pure invention. Again, a look at the whole suggests otherwise. Plato is both comprehensive and exacting in his physical description of Atlantis. It seems unlikely that a philosopher, whose main interest was culture, would take such trouble unless he felt a need to be true to a core of fact.

The original culture of Atlantis was presented as orderly and generally along the lines of Socrates' ideal society. Laws were respected. Religious rites, including the sacrifice of a bull to Poseidon, were duly performed. Harmony was maintained between humankind and the gods of the Greek pantheon. This harmony derived from the fact that the early rulers of Atlantis descended directly from Poseidon, and retained his god-like qualities. With the passage of time and generations the divine element was diluted by mortal qualities. Human traits came to the forefront, resulting in the pursuit of fame, fortune and power.

The gods became angry at the degeneration of Atlantean society. The chief god, Zeus, decreed the punishment of Atlantis. Plato abandons the dialogue just as Critias is about to detail Zeus' instructions regarding Atlantis to the lesser gods. The parallels with Athens of Plato's time are obvious, although to what extent they may have slanted his telling of the story of Atlantis is unknown. If Plato's intent was to use the fate of Atlantis to raise alarm among the Athenians about their own future, then it made little sense to use a purely fictional metaphor. An example firmly grounded in historical fact would make a far more convincing argument.

Plato went to some lengths to insist that Atlantis and its people were real. Writers in antiquity, with access to sources now lost, addressed the question. One was Crantor of Cilicia, a philosopher who followed Plato by a century and wrote commentary on Plato's works. He reported that he travelled to Egypt and inspected Stelae validating the tale told to Solon by the Egyptian priests. Plutarch, in his *Parallel Lives,* gives the names of two Egyptian priests, Sonchis of Sais and Psenophis of Heliopolis, who told Solon the story of Atlantis. The later Roman writer Pliny the Elder cited Atlantis as a source of tin. Other ancient writers weighed in on the subject of Atlantis, but offered few specifics and no evidence.

If Atlantis did exist, then its destruction must have left some residue. Nothing vanishes completely. Even the most violent asteroid impacts, far exceeding the most powerful thermonuclear blast, left traces that remain visible tens of millions of years later. Further, the destruction would not have happened in a vacuum. The forces involved must have resulted in devastation in the surrounding area. The sudden loss of a robust trading partner would have been felt by Atlantis' counterparties and noted in their archives.

If we are to find the residue of Atlantis today, Plato's tale offers only a general level of help. There is a sense he was writing about a real place. His descriptions are detailed and conceivably accurate, but his chronology and geography are muddled. We have no way to separate fact from misunderstanding, mistranslation, embellishment, philosophy and pure nonsense. There are only two real clues.

The first clue is that the tale of Atlantis originated in Egypt. If true the story must refer to a place known to the Egyptians. Since Atlantis was an island, it must be located in a sea familiar to the Egyptians. The most likely area is the Mediterranean/Aegean complex. It was well known to the Egyptians and contained numerous islands with significant populations. The other possibility is the Red Sea. Archaeologists have excavated an ancient Egyptian harbor facility at Mersa Gawassis, on Egypt's eastern coast. The presence of the harbor corroborates documents detailing Egyptian trade on the Red Sea. The absence of islands large enough to support a civilization makes the Red Sea a less likely location.

The second clue is that the destruction of Atlantis must have been an event of sufficient scope and scale to be memorialized by the Egyptians. Egyptian records go back not much farther than 3,000 BC. That establishes a time frame. The Eastern Mediterranean region is among the most seismically active in the world. Destructive earthquakes were not uncommon. We will need to find an event that far exceeded the norm in magnitude. We will also need to find evidence of the destructive floods described by Plato.

THE ISLAND OF
SAINT IRENE

The late Nineteenth Century AD saw unprecedented archaeological activity in the Eastern Mediterranean. European expeditions trekked into the forbidding wastes of Egypt and excavated the remains of a forgotten civilization. Painstaking translation of hieroglyphic writing uncovered the history of a Bronze Age empire. Egypt, long considered nothing more than a backwater destination for Arab traders, had once held sway from the fourth cataract of the Nile in the south and, under Pharaoh Thutmoses III, fought its way to the Euphrates River some twelve hundred miles to the north.

Other locations yielded equally stunning finds. In Turkey a German amateur, Heinrich Schliemann, found the legendary city of Troy, known from Homer's epic *Iliad*. The city was thought by most scholars of Schliemann's time to be only a mythical setting for a fictional tale. Agamemnon's capital of Mycenae was uncovered in Greece and gave its name to the Mycenaean Empire, which we will explore in a coming chapter. In 1900 AD the British archaeologist Sir Arthur Evans began excavation at the ancient city of Knossos on the island of Crete, forty miles south of the Greek mainland. He unearthed a civilization to which he applied the name Minoan, after King Minos and the half man-half bull Minotaur of Greek mythology.

It was not long before observers began to note similarities between the emerging knowledge of Minoan culture and Plato's description of Atlantean society. In particular Minoan frescoes of bull leaping brought to mind Plato's mention of the Atlanteans' sacrifice of a bull to Poseidon. The reality was that ceremonies involving bulls were common among widely scattered societies during the Bronze Age. Similar rituals persist in the metropolitan bull rings of modern day Spain and Mexico. That did not hinder the search for other connections to Plato's Atlantis.

In 1965 AD the Greek archaeologist Spyridon Marinatos began excavating a Minoan city now called Akrotiri, located on the Aegean Island of Santorini, some sixty miles north and east of Crete. Santorini is one of a number of picturesque islands dotting the Aegean Sea off the east coast of Greece. Satellite photographs show them laid out in a vaguely linear sprawl, sun-baked and dun colored against the azure of the water. In reality they are the peaks of an undersea mountain range. Santorini's mountain is a volcano.

The city of Akrotiri had been entombed by a massive eruption that destroyed part of the original island. The eruption was the latest in a cycle of eruptions stretching back hundreds of thousands of years. Prior volcanic activity had left a central dome and the concentric rings of two crater walls protruding from the sea. The result closely matched Plato's description of the rings of water and of land that guarded the central hill of Atlantis. These were destroyed in the eruption that entombed Akrotiri.

As further corroboration, the only entrance to the sea-filled craters from the main body of the Aegean had lain between the small island of Aspronisi and the main island. This closely matched Plato's description of a long, narrow entrance to Atlantis' harbor.

The entombed city of Akrotiri was perfectly preserved. It lay just as it had on the day of the eruption. Its size and level of finish left no doubt it had been constructed by an advanced civilization. Exquisite artwork was still visible on the walls, depicting the same themes as Minoan Crete, and described in Plato's dialogues. In the city's prime a traveler approaching from the sea would have seen limestone exteriors shimmering in the Mediterranean sun, creating at least the illusion of a beckoning utopia. Santorini became the leading candidate for Plato's lost continent.

Santorini is a modern name for the island. The name anglicizes to Saint Irene. In earlier times it was referred to as Thera. That name comes from the commander of a Spartan garrison established on the island centuries after the collapse of Minoan civilization. We don't know what the Minoans called either the island or the city we now call Akrotiri. Or what they called themselves for that matter. The Minoans were a literate society, but the writing they left behind has so far defied decipherment.

Sir Arthur Evans named Minoan writing Linear A. The term linear simply refers to the fact that the characters foot to a horizontal line. It appears similar to, and in fact shares some symbols with, Mycenaean Linear B, which we can read. Linear B is a combination of syllabic and pictographic. The symbols refer to syllables rather that individual letters as is the case in this book, and are supplemented by pictures to represent certain entities (e.g. cattle or sheep). It is assumed that Linear A is also a combination of syllabic and pictographic. That does not imply that similar symbols mean the same thing in both schemes of writing.

All writing can be broken into two parts. The first is the scheme of symbols used. The second is the underlying language the symbols represent. The same arrangement of symbols can mean something in one language and nothing in another. Take for example the five letter group *caxap*. An English speaker would probably pronounce it *kak-sap* and dismiss it as nonsense. There is no such word. A Russian speaker would pronounce it *sa-char* and recognize it as meaning sugar. Conversely the meaning conveyed by a white board covered with algebraic notation might be understood by mathematicians regardless of what language they spoke.

We are able to read Linear B because translators recognized the underlying language as an early form of Greek. Scholars have not been able to identify the language underlying Linear A. Evidence that it differed from Greek can be found in the Ninth Book of Homer's *Odyssey*. Speaking of Crete, Homer says each of the several races of the island has its own language. First is Achaean, referring to the form of Greek spoken by the Mycenaeans and written in Linear B, then the language of the genuine Cretans (Minoans) which would have been written in Linear A.

Approximately four of every five of the symbols in Linear A are unique. Substituting values for matching symbols from Linear B has failed to produce any comprehensible text. A proposed system of Linear A numbers, including weights and fractions, has been worked out based on Linear B analogs. This enshrines the Minoans among the mathematically sophisticated civilizations of their time, but provides no historical narrative.

A further difficulty in deciphering Linear A lies in the limited number of examples available. Only about 1,400 inscriptions have been found. They contain fewer than 7,500 symbols. For comparison, the single page you are reading has about 2,000 letters or spaces for letters. All of the known Linear A writing could fit onto four pages, with room to spare.

None of the known examples are in multilingual format. A multilingual is a document, such as a proclamation, diplomatic communication or trade agreement, written in multiple languages, at least one of which we can read. The best known example is the trilingual *Rosetta Stone,* a decree honoring the Pharaoh Ptolemy V in 196 BC, written in Egyptian hieroglyphic, demotic and Greek. It was discovered accidentally during the construction of military fortifications around the turn of the Nineteenth Century AD. Without this stroke of luck we might still be struggling with the process of translating Egyptian hieroglyphics. Even with the *Rosetta Stone,* translation required knowledge of a significant number of place and personal names, and involved use of the considerable trove of Egyptian writing collected over centuries.

Absent intelligible writing, we will have to look at the human remains and artifacts the Minoans left behind, as well as the writings of contemporary cultures, to learn what we can of them.

The best information we have as to the origin of the Minoans comes from genetic studies involving collection, classification and comparison of DNA from Minoan skeletal remains. DNA, renowned for applications in law enforcement and genealogical research, is an acronym for Deoxyribo Nucleic Acid. In simple terms it is the instruction set used to construct and maintain the human body.

DNA exists in segments called genes. The genes are made up of chains of four nucleotides; adenine, cytosine, guanine and thymine (designated by the leading letters A, C, G and T in gene maps). There are about three billion pairs of these chemical building blocks in the human body. A typical gene will contain around a thousand nucleotides in a combination that tells the body which proteins to manufacture. These proteins determine visible properties like eye and hair color and invisible ones that control the physical aspects of our being. Although each person's DNA is unique, the fact that DNA is inherited means that people related by blood share some DNA passed down from common ancestors.

The DNA molecule is packaged into thread-like structures called chromosomes, of which there are twenty three pairs. There are two types of chromosomes, labeled X and Y. Men differ from women in that they have both X and Y chromosomes, while women have only X chromosomes. Male DNA is referred to as simply DNA. Female DNA is referred to as mitochondrial DNA, usually abbreviated as mtDNA. Both forms are subject to random mutation over time. The mutations are passed from parents to children. Mutations are classified into sequences called haplogroups and smaller sequences called haplotypes. A population sharing a common haplogroup also shares a common ancestor, although perhaps hundreds of generations removed.

Traces of ancestral DNA become diluted as successive generations intermarry with neighboring populations. Over time the identity of populations becomes less distinct. Establishing the source of a population required that laboratory analysis of DNA escalate from the individual to the industrial level. Laboratory facilities had to be expanded and procedures modified to permit the analysis of large numbers of samples. This is a recent development that has provided a more accurate picture of how the ancient world came to be populated.

The Human Genome Project has identified a broad spectrum of haplogroups and provided them with alpha-numeric designators. Studies of male DNA among Minoans on Crete showed a high frequency of the haplogroup J2a-M410, which suggests migration from Western Anatolia, modern day Turkey. A later study of mitochondrial DNA established that about three quarters of the Minoan population on Crete originated from Western Anatolia and the Aegean region, with other contributions from areas of Europe. No similarity was found with Egyptian or Libyan populations. This suggests the Egyptians would have considered the Minoans foreigners, assuming the Egyptians knew the Minoans existed.

Minoan civilization flourished during the Mediterranean Bronze Age, from about 2700 BC to about 1600 BC, on Crete and several Aegean islands. After that it appears to have existed either subordinate to or in conjunction with the Mycenaean civilization of nearby Greece, not dying out entirely until about 1100 BC. Ample evidence exists to establish that the Egyptians were not only aware of the Minoans but regularly interacted with them. Examples of Minoan art and ceramics have been found at multiple sites in Egypt, suggesting either a Minoan commercial presence in the country or at least strong cultural exchange. Artifacts imported from Egypt to Crete have been used by archaeologists to establish a Minoan chronology.

We also have a time capsule in the form of a ship that sank off the Turkish village of Uluburun around 1300 BC. The ship was a substantial vessel fifty feet in length. In order for its operation to be economically feasible it would have needed large cargos and regular ports of call. In addition to cargo traceable to the Minoans, the ship contained the scarab of the Egyptian Queen Nefertiti.

Written records associated with Minoan goods found in various parts of the Eastern Mediterranean mention a country called Caphtor. This may be what the Minoans called their homeland. Judeo-Christian scripture (Jeremiah 47:4) cites the Philistines as remnants of the land of Caphtor. The Philistines will be examined in a later chapter. They were forcibly resettled in Canaan by the Egyptians after the defeat of a Mycenaean invasion of Egypt in 1178 BC.

In order to establish the Minoans as candidates for Plato's Atlanteans we need to determine whether mention of the Minoans existed in Egyptian records. This is not as straightforward as it may seem. Egyptian hieroglyphics are notoriously difficult to read and interpret. Part of the difficulty comes from their use of terms that were universally understood at the time but are now lost.

Imagine the plight of an archaeologist 3,000 years in the future, when the English language and its American idiom have long been forgotten, excavating the remains of a Twenty First Century AD city and trying to translate the character set *MTA*. The poor scholar would have no way to know that it was not a word but an acronym for Metropolitan Transit

Authority. And no way to know that it had any relation to the ruins of the intricate urban rail system the work crews were unearthing.

An example from Egyptian times is the word *Kheti*, discovered in a trove of diplomatic correspondence. It seemed to refer to a nation or a people, but no one had heard of any such place or civilization. Meanwhile, in Anatolia, archaeologists were uncovering the remains of an empire that called itself *Rulers of the Land of Hatti*. Eventually the two were put together and connected with the Biblical Hittites, whom we will encounter later. History had lost track of an entire empire for more than 2,000 years.

When we examine the Egyptian records for mention of the Minoans, we need to be mindful that Minoan is a name adopted solely for the convenience of modern scholars, and further that references to Minoan civilization may be oblique.

The hieroglyphic scheme of writing presents its own difficulties. Characters do not correspond to the individual letters in any alphabetic language, but rather represent sounds or concepts. The characters representing sounds can correspond to groups of one, two or three letters in English (monoliteral, biliteral and triliteral). All of the letter groups are consonants. No vowels as we understand them were used, although a couple of letters we think of as vowels turn up occasionally as consonants.

If that were not confusing enough, the signs representing concepts can be obscure. The verb to drink may be represented by a human figure with hand to mouth followed by three wavy lines representing water. The wavy lines exist in spite of the fact that there was a five character hieroglyph for *inu,* the Egyptian word for water. To further the confusion, *inu* also referred to spoils of war, and a second five character hieroglyph represented *Inu,* a goddess. To their credit, scholars have been able to wade through these and a litany of other peculiarities to locate mention of the Minoans.

An example comes from the correspondence of Fourteenth Century BC Pharaoh Amenhotep III. A hieroglyphic *kftw* appears in a reference interpreted as the *secret islands north of Asia.* Insertion of vowels according to modern convention for ease of reading produces a transliteration of *Kaftor.* The term convention is used loosely. As an example, modern transliterations of the name of the island of Crete can appear as *Keftu, Keftiu* or *Keftiou* (a word generally taken to mean *islands in the middle of the sea*). For further confirmation, the Egyptian correspondence also calls out Minoan cities by name, including Knossos and Phaistos, two of the most important urban centers on Crete at the time.

One thing the correspondence does not mention is the aftermath of the volcanic devastation of Santorini. For this we will need to look to a massive, inscribed granite stone called the *Tempest Stela*. This effort will entail overcoming its own set of difficulties. The Stela is broken and incomplete. Its date of origin is controversial. The inscriptions it contains have been subjected to multiple interpretations. The subject is complex enough to require extensive consideration. We will postpone detailed discussion to a later and more relevant chapter.

Once we have met the requirement that the Egyptians knew of and recorded Minoan civilization, we can examine the physical remains of Santorini to see if any of Plato's description of Atlantis is corroborated. The island does have springs of hot and cold water. The entombed city of Akrotiri does generally match Plato's description of a shimmering home to an advanced society. Major Minoans cities appear to have included water management systems that delivered filtered drinking water, provided bathing facilities and carried away waste. To gain an appreciation of how advanced indoor plumbing and urban sewage disposal were in 1600 BC we need only remember that Americans were still running for their outhouses as little as 200 years ago. And that the streets of London reeked of horse manure and urine throughout the comparatively recent reign of Queen Victoria, the zenith of the British Empire.

Additional corroboration comes from a large fresco discovered in a house in Akrotiri. The fresco is detailed enough to show a fleet of ships coming to harbor, varying in size from small vessels suitable for coastal trading to one estimated at 120 feet in length and square rigged for open sea travel.

Since the fresco is Minoan there has been a tendency to see the vessels as the product of Minoan shipwrights and the Minoans as a hardy, seafaring people. This is not necessarily the case. In 1957 AD the United States Air Force published a family photograph of its air fleet, possibly the modern equivalent of the Minoan fresco. Included was the British designed Canberra bomber, which was later deployed in the Vietnam conflict.

The Uluburun shipwreck illustrates a possibility from Minoan times. Although it carried some Minoan sourced cargo, the timber used in its construction indicated it may have been built in Canaan. Even if the ships were operated by the Minoan merchants, they did not necessarily carry Minoan crews. A good portion of today's sea trade is dependent on crews made up of expatriate Filipino sailors, regardless of vessel ownership or flag. There is also the possibility mentioned by Plato, that the fresco portrayed visiting vessels from other trading powers.

The realistic nature of the Akrotiri fresco suggests that it was intended as a slice of daily life. The variety, detail and proportionality of the vessels appear to be accurate. The elevation and coloration of the harbor are consistent with what we do know of the island's geography and buildings. It seems reasonable to accept the Akrotiri fresco as a portrait of Santorini as it was before the eruption.

The fresco is not a precise match to Plato's description of Atlantis' harbor, but it does show similarity in that Akrotiri was part of a maritime trading network. The entrance to Santorini's harbor was narrow, as Plato described it. Prior volcanic activity had left concentric rings of land and water. Overall, Plato's description of Atlantis appears to have originated with someone who had seen the Island of Saint Irene before the eruption, when it was a fully operational component of the far flung Minoan commercial complex.

To merit a place in the Egyptian archives the eruption that destroyed Santorini needed to be exceptional, even by the lofty standards of the seismically active Eastern Mediterranean. The modern view of volcanic eruption is filtered through the prism of Hollywood imagination and television news coverage of actual events. While some of the special effects and news footage have appeared spectacular, we have not had a comparable eruption within the life span of motion picture and television cameras. The 1991 AD eruption of Mount Pinatubo in the Philippines was a full order of magnitude less than Santorini. The 1980 AD eruption of Mount St. Helens in Washington State was two full orders of magnitude less.

Scientists studying the effects of eruptions over eons past have classified them according to explosive force. The largest is the super volcano. The minimum threshold for super volcano status is 1,000 cubic kilometers of ejecta. One thousand cubic kilometers is equivalent to a cube of rock and debris ten kilometers on a side, ripped loose from the earth and blown skyward in a single blast. For comparison, this is more than 2,500 times the volume of ejecta involved in the eruption of Mount St. Helens. That eruption blew the top 1,300 feet of the mountain off and sent an ash cloud 15 miles into the air, where powerful winds aloft spread it over twelve states. Although the eruption that devastated Santorini fell short of super volcano status, it was still one of the most powerful ever to have occurred.

In addition to dwarfing any other seismic event in the region during written memory it also produced tsunamis that meet Plato's criteria of devastating floods. On Crete the primary coastal towns of Katsamsa, Amniso and Agii Theodotis were destroyed. Archaeologists have found evidence of severe infrastructure damage further inland. A passage in later Greek drama suggests that a massive tidal wave struck the east coast of Greece. The Tsunami, as well as eyewitness reports from other locations, would have reached Egypt. Information thus accumulated may have become the core of the tale of the destruction of Atlantis that made its way to Plato.

Ejecta from the Santorini eruption reached stratospheric levels. In addition to smothering ash it contained a witch's brew of toxic chemicals. The ash would settle quickly, but worse poisons would circle the globe. The consequences exceeded the scope of anything even suspected by Plato or the Egyptians.

To understand the global consequences of the Santorini eruption it will be helpful to take a basic course in how volcanoes work. It is not as simple as presented in middle school science text books.

VOLCANIC ERUPTION 101

Volcanic eruptions are rare and sensational events. They routinely attract television news coverage. To this fact we are indebted for our general sense of the power and the visible destructive forces involved in eruptions. Video footage of glowing lava crawling downward in viscous rivers testifies eloquently to the hellish temperatures below. The lahar, a moving mass of mud and debris, crushes everything in its path. Ash clouds rising miles into the sky make a spectacular backdrop for reports of civil aviation disruption. Tsunami flooding is telecast in the context of massive infrastructure damage. Cell phone video of fleeing residents and coverage of frantic rescue efforts add a human dimension that allows us to cast ourselves, however briefly, into the role of the victims as they see the lives they have built up over years of toil vanish before their eyes.

At best television coverage is a vicarious and transient experience. The whole event is edited into a sixty second time frame. It is accompanied by a scripted voice-over from the on-scene reporter or the studio anchor person. As soon as the eruption has been milked for all the available sensation, the coverage is archived and forgotten. Lost is the fact that the eruption is only one phase of an ongoing seismic process that neither begins with the explosive event nor ends as soon as the lava cools and the ash settles.

In order to understand the impact of the Santorini eruption, we will need to understand the full volcanic cycle, including the short and long term chemical consequences when reactive elements are exposed to intense heat and great pressure. Equally important is the environment in which the event took place. The Santorini eruption occurred in direct contact with one large fluid body, the Aegean/Mediterranean Sea complex. It ejected a substantial portion of its output into another large fluid body, the Earth's atmosphere. Both fluid bodies played critical roles in transmitting the destructive consequences of the eruption.

The traditional view of a volcano is of a mountain sitting above an underground pool of molten rock called magma. The top of the mountain holds an opening in the form of a crater, or caldera. From there a tubular shaft runs down through the solid rock of the mountain and the Earth's crust to the pool of magma, something on the order of a drinking straw plunged into a milkshake. An eruption occurs when pressure builds deep in the Earth and magma shoots up the straw and out of the crater.

This oversimplification ignores several critical facts. The straw is really a labyrinth of subterranean fissure. The solid rock of the mountain is not uniform in either physical properties or chemical composition. The magma has its own chemical composition, and reacts with different layers and pockets of rock as it wends its way through the labyrinth.

In particular, chemical reactions will be important in our exploration of the results of the Santorini eruption. These reactions create the stew of ash and toxic aerosols that are ejected into the atmosphere to be spread on the winds. No two volcanic events produce exactly the same composition of ejecta. Volcanic residue can be traced to a specific eruption no matter how far it is found from the source.

If we are to understand the eruption process and its consequences, we need to trace it from its roots. The initial driver of volcanic action is a phenomenon called subduction. The land beneath our feet, and beneath the oceans, exists as massive tectonic plates. These plates are in constant motion, although they may move as little as two centimeters per year. At the line of contact between two plates moving in opposite directions, something has to give. The cooler, and therefore denser, oceanic plate will move under the warmer continental plate in a process called subduction. This is the phenomenon that produces the Pacific Ocean's notorious ring of fire.

The oceanic plate carries hydrous minerals and clays. These break down as the plate descends and release a large quantity of water which, at the prevailing high temperature and pressure, becomes a supercritical fluid. The supercritical water rises into the mantle rock where it lowers the pressure, and therefore the melting point, of the rock. The reduced melting point combines with great subterranean heat to produce magma.

In most cases the liquid magma cannot rise because it has solid rock above it. Instead it is forced to travel laterally until it encounters an exploitable fault in the rock through which heat and pressure can force it to rise. In addition to upward pressure, the magma column also exerts pressure against the walls of the fault. The force of the moving magma is often enough to displace segments of rock adjoining the fault, creating earthquakes in the area of the volcano.

The likelihood of earthquakes preceding the Santorini eruption is notable for two reasons. First, it conforms to Plato's account of earthquakes involved in the destruction of Atlantis. Second, it provides a possible explanation of an anomaly found, or rather not found, in the entombed city of Akrotiri. In other volcanically entombed cities, most famously Pompey and Herculaneum, a large number of human casualties were discovered, either as remains or as hollows left in the entombing tufa. No such casualties have been identified at Akrotiri. One theory is that the Minoan inhabitants of Santorini fled the island in advance of the eruption due to the increasing frequency and ferocity of these earthquakes. Once out of danger, they told of their experience, leading to the belief that earthquakes rather than a volcanic eruption had devastated the island.

That theory is unproven, and runs counter to normal human behavior in proximity to volcanoes. People living in the vicinity of a volcano become accustomed to earthquakes after a few shocks have been felt and nothing serious has happened. They continue with their routine rather than abandon the lives and wealth it has taken generations to build up.

That reluctance persists even in modern times. The city of Goma in Central Africa, home to about two million people, lies in a volcanic danger zone. The residents seem resigned to the peril. When interviewed one said, presumably in reference to the rich volcanic soil in the region, that the mountain brings life and the mountain brings death. When Mount St.

Helens erupted in 1980 AD, the authorities had no mandatory evacuation order in place. 57 people were killed by the eruption or by the resulting debris flow. Some of the victims had come to the mountain specifically to view it, or to photograph it venting steam.

An alternative explanation for the abandonment of Akrotiri also originates with the behavior of rising magma. Aided by heat and pressure, gasses formed in the magma chamber can vent upward to the surface. Some of the resulting sulfur based gasses are recognizably toxic. If the venting process replaces them more quickly than they can dissipate, the area becomes uninhabitable. A non-sulfur based gas, carbon dioxide, is more subtle and persistent. Carbon dioxide is part of the output of normal mammalian respiration. In the form of dry ice it is used to create theatrical effects of smoke and fog, and is routinely inhaled by cast members without ill effect. The lethal property of the gas arises when it is concentrated to the point that it upsets the normal mix of nitrogen and oxygen in the atmosphere.

To cite a modern example, the pressurization systems in airliners have to take this effect into account. Fresh air is blown into the cabin at a constant rate. Cabin pressure is maintained by regulating the rate at which the air is exhausted. If air were simply blown in and left stagnant, like blowing up a balloon, the carbon dioxide exhaled by the passengers would concentrate to the point where everyone in the cabin would suffocate within thirty minutes.

Carbon dioxide vented as a result of seismic activity below ground is heavier than air. Gravity would concentrate it in low lying areas, displacing the normal atmosphere and suffocating everything that relied on respiration for life. Such an event actually happened at Lake Nyos in Cameroon in 1986 AD. There was no detectable volcanic activity to serve as a warning. A massive venting of carbon dioxide from a subterranean chamber blanketed the area, suffocating all life. Similar accumulations of the invisible and undetectable gas may have occurred in the low areas around the Santorini volcano, particularly in the lower chambers of Akrotiri. Such an event would have made the area around the volcano uninhabitable, forcing the residents to bury their dead and evacuate prior to the eruption.

Other chemical reactions were instrumental in determining the power of the Santorini eruption. Rising magma reacts with silica-rich layers of rock it encounters on its upward journey. The magma thickens and partially crystallizes into viscous goo that sticks to the walls of the fissures acting as a conduit for the magma, trapping the magma below in any chamber that is convenient. Immense pressure builds until the trapped magma is expelled with eruptive force. If magma took only one route upward, the picture would be fairly simple. In reality pressurized magma forces its way into any available fissure and may find multiple conduits. Some of these pathways may pass through silica-deficient rock, leaving only gravity, friction and the constriction of the fissure to oppose the upward pressure. This can lead to a complex pattern of eruption, such as we see at Santorini.

Magma is an important component of volcanic activity, but the pressure behind it is the driving force. The buildup of pressure is slow and not directly observable, so there is some element of theory in the explanation of how it happens. The prevailing thinking can be summarized as follows. Over time the subduction process creates more and more magma that is forced up into the sticky goo in the chamber above. The heat of the rising magma melts some of the crystalline structure of the goo and produces volatile fluids, much of it in the form of water bubbles. The bubbles can force the partially melted goo upward to create small eruptions. Pressure at the top of the chamber drops, so the bubbles of water can expand rapidly. A sudden jolt of rising bubbles can trigger a massive eruption.

The Santorini eruption ejected an estimated 24 cubic miles of material. This is approximately four times the estimated amount ejected by the powerful eruption that split the Pacific Island of Krakatoa in 1883 AD, an event heard 3,600 miles away in Australia. In modern terms it is the equivalent of blasting the 22.7 square mile island of Manhattan into flying fragments and leaving a hole more than a mile deep in its place.

The Santorini eruption left a 200 foot thick layer of volcanic tephra overlying the island. That is the height of an eighteen story office building. The tephra occurs in distinct layers, allowing analysis of the phases of the eruption. The first phase was a characterized by a relatively thin deposit of tephra. It was probably the precursor eruption expected in advance of major activity. The inhabitants were gone by this time; otherwise they would have been entombed and their remains discovered by modern excavators.

We have no insight into how much the Minoans knew about volcanoes. It is possible they occupied Santorini as a calculated risk to take advantage of its location and sheltered deep water harbor. A modern example is the Hawaiian Islands. The island chain is in fact the tips of five undersea mountains rising in some cases over 30,000 feet above the sea bed, higher than Mount Everest. The mountains reached that height as a result of eons of accumulation of volcanic ejecta. Hawaii's location made it an ideal refueling stop for trans-Pacific air travel. Its protected harbor sheltered elements of the U.S. Pacific fleet. It blossomed into a vacation paradise involving massive investment in lodging and amenities. Tourists flock there annually, some to view the volcanic activity.

The only injuries from the last eruptive event in 2018 AD occurred when a sightseeing boat was struck by volcanic ejecta. The low intensity and extended duration of the event, combined with careful monitoring by volcanologists using drone cameras and state of the art sensors, prevented any fatalities. Had the eruption occurred with the force of the Santorini event, in the absence of modern technology, the loss of life could have been staggering. Under any circumstances a comparable tsunami would have obliterated all the major seaports along the U.S. west coast.

In the case of Santorini, the major eruption occurred in four phases. The first deposited 23 feet of ash and pumice, burying manmade structures (Akrotiri) without significant damage. The second and third phases involved lava and possibly some debris flow. Any structures not protectively buried in the first phase would have been destroyed. It is possible that tsunami activity may have been generated during these phases. The craters left from eruptions thousands of years earlier began to collapse. The fourth phase completed the caldera collapse and initiated massive debris flows.

Had the Santorini eruption occurred in a vacuum, its devastation would have been localized. The adjoining compressible fluid media, the Aegean/Mediterranean Sea complex and the Earth's atmosphere, transmitted both the force and the ejecta of the eruption in ways that would profoundly alter the course of history.

Debris flows and the collapse of the caldera resulted in a mega-tsunami. A tsunami is a series of seismic waves resulting from a large displacement of water. Tsunamis are associated with major bodies of water, such as seas or oceans. They are characterized by a long wavelength, the distance from crest to crest, which can be as much as 120 miles, and by high velocity, which can reach 500 miles per hour, approximately the speed of a trans-oceanic jetliner. Due to the distance between crests, the height of each crest is relatively low, about three feet, and the wave cannot be felt by ships at sea. The mass and velocity of water is not evident until the wave collides with a stationary land mass.

The waterborne force of a tsunami is magnified as the trough of the wave approaches impact with land. Water is drawn back from coastal coves and harbors as the tidal wave approaches. The accumulated mass of the drawn up water together with that of the seismic wave is hurled onto the land with destructive force. Water finds its way into every crevice, leaving no element of human infrastructure untouched. It moves faster than any human can run and recedes within minutes, carrying massive amounts of debris with it.

The tsunami would have crossed the Mediterranean to the coasts of Egypt and Libya as well as impacting the Eastern Mediterranean coast of Canaan. The north coast of Crete, less than 70 miles from Santorini, shows traces of damage up to 500 hundred feet above sea level The inevitable loss of ships, harbor facilities and personnel experienced in operating a maritime merchant network would have been a particularly damaging blow for a trading culture like the Minoans.

A sophisticated trading network defines the world in which it functions. People who mine and manufacture need not concern themselves that their land produces little in the way of staple crops. They can trade their output for whatever they require. Similarly, resource poor agricultural areas can exchange their surplus food to offset shortcomings in raw materials and finished goods. Specialization and interdependence become the order of the day.

It was probably location and economy of movement that put the Minoan civilization at the hub of the Eastern Mediterranean trade network. According to the later Romans, who constructed what was arguably the finest road network in the ancient world, transporting cargo by sea cost only one twentieth of what it cost to move the same cargo overland.

The Minoans had developed as an island civilization, which required the expertise, infrastructure and ships to support maritime transport.

The simultaneous destruction of ports at Santorini, on Crete and throughout the Eastern Mediterranean crippled the prevailing trade network. With cargo movement abruptly curtailed, the specialized society which depended upon efficient logistics provided by Minoan mastery of the Aegean and Mediterranean fell victim to the interaction between the Santorini eruption and the Seas.

The damage done by ash, debris and aerosols ejected into the atmosphere is more widespread as a result of not being contained by land masses. The ejecta are blown as high as the stratosphere, estimated as high as 22 miles in the case of Santorini. They are borne not only on surface winds but also on high level winds referred to as the jet stream, which can approach velocities of 250 miles per hour. Lower level winds are subject to change in direction according to temperature differences in adjoining land masses, which can create areas of high and low atmospheric pressure. The higher level jet stream is driven by Coriolis force resulting from the rotation of the Earth on it axis. In the latitudes near Santorini it makes its way consistently west to east, although its precise path varies greatly over time. The combined upper and lower winds drove the ejecta from the Santorini eruption mainly eastward.

On the island of Anafi, 27 miles east of Santorini, ash deposits as deep as ten feet have been found. Lesser deposits traceable to the Santorini eruption have been found on the Anatolian mainland to the east. Ash fall can choke agriculture and, in significant quantity, change watercourses. Volcanic ash is highly visible. It is given more credit than it deserves for the long term damage done by volcanic eruption.

A greater impact comes from the aerosols ejected by the volcano. Many of these are sulfurous in nature, including sulfuric acid. The overall mass is referred to as a stratospheric sulfate aerosol veil. The effect of the veil is to reflect sunlight away from the ground. Unlike the transient volcanic ash, which settles out of the air fairly quickly, aerosols are persistent. They last long enough to create what is called volcanic winter. Temperatures plunge, crops fail and livestock dies. Civilizations must adapt. Those that do not are doomed to collapse.

The aerosols are blown high enough to be carried on the jet stream, and their impact has global reach. The 1815 AD eruption of Mount Tambora in the Indonesian Archipelago, comparable in Volcanic Explosivity Index with the Santorini eruption, produced a volcanic winter around the world in 1815/16 AD. Snow fell in June in Albany, New York. Livestock perished in New England and crops throughout the United States were ruined. Crop failures in Europe drove food prices up sharply. Riots, arson and looting plagued many major cities. The monsoons in China and India were disrupted, leading to massive agricultural failures in Asia.

We have nothing like the sensational newspaper headlines of the Nineteenth Century AD to help us assess the global impact of the Santorini eruption. We will need to rely on contemporary writing, later histories, archaeological finds and technical analysis. In order to match the Santorini eruption with global events of the past we will need to know both when it happened and what the world looked like at that time.

THE QUESTION OF WHEN

The date of the Santorini eruption has been a bone of contention for decades. Various authorities have championed dates ranging from 1642 BC to 1450 BC. Each cites apparently valid evidence to support the proposed date. None of the evidence appears to reconcile. Our task will be to sort through the contradictions and confusion and come to the most defensible approximation of the date of the Santorini eruption. To accomplish this we will need to understand the applicable methods of dating and the strengths and shortcomings of each.

Ice Cores

The Earth's glaciers, in particular the stable glaciers in Greenland and Antarctica, grow in annual cycles. Wind and gravity deposit each year's residue, including volcanic ash, on the surface of the ice. Following snowfall entombs that residue. The process is repeated year after year. Scientists can drill a core out of the ice and read from the layers of deposits in the core a rough history of weather and other impacts on an annual basis going back many thousand years.

Reading the data locked in the ice is not a trivial undertaking. Ice cores present murky bands of coloration that require skill, experience and scientific analysis to properly interpret. The difficulty of reading increases with age. The layers become more difficult to discern deeper in the ice. Verification has to rely on geochemistry, electrical conductivity and rarely, where available, on the decay rate of the isotope Uranium-235.

Ice core interpretation is an evolving discipline. The Santorini eruption is a case in point. Evidence of a large volcanic eruption was found in a Greenland ice core and dated to 1642 BC. The Santorini eruption came immediately to mind. The ice core deposit was cited as evidence for the year of the Santorini eruption. Subsequent analysis of the deposit established that it was not chemically consistent with ejecta from Santorini. It is now thought to relate to an eruption of Mount Aniakchak in Alaska.

Without specific knowledge of weather patterns at the time of the Santorini eruption we don't know whether ejecta are likely to have reached the Greenland glacial mass. Current survey is far from comprehensive. Nor is it likely to progress rapidly. Drilling to a depth going back three and a half thousand years involves a multi-year encampment on a remote glacier. A single drilling expedition may involve years of planning and coordination, expensive equipment and daunting logistics. Ice core dating may someday pinpoint the year of the Santorini eruption. The current scope of knowledge will not be helpful.

Isotope Analysis

Our world is made up of elements. The basic unit of an element is an atom. Each atom consists of a nucleus containing a specific number of positively charged particles called protons and an equal number of uncharged particles called neutrons. Surrounding the nucleus are negatively charged electrons existing in a probability cloud at various energy levels. The nature of the element is determined by the number of protons. Carbon, for example, has six protons and six neutrons resulting in a nuclear particle count of twelve. Nitrogen has seven protons and seven neutrons for a count of fourteen.

Occasionally forms of an element will be found in nature with an unequal count of protons and neutrons. These are called isotopes. These are generally unstable and tend to decay back to a stable state at a known rate. The known rate of decay of an isotope of carbon underlies the process generally known as radiocarbon dating.

The Earth's atmosphere is made up of almost 80% nitrogen. The atmosphere is also under constant bombardment by cosmic rays, tiny packets of energy potent enough to disrupt the nucleus of an atom. Rarely a collision between an atomic nucleus and one of these packets of energy will knock a neutron loose and send it into another nucleus, where it knocks a proton loose and replaces it. When this replacement occurs in the nucleus of a nitrogen atom, the result is the creation of a carbon atom, by reducing the proton count from seven to six. The neutron count increases to eight, so the total nuclear particle count remains fourteen, resulting in an isotope called carbon-14.

Carbon-14 has a half life of 5,730 years. That means half of it will decay back to a stable state, essentially cease to exist, in that amount of time. New carbon-14 is constantly being created in the atmosphere during the decay process. The relative rates of creation and decay keep the ratio of carbon-14 to stable carbon relatively constant. Earth's life forms are carbon based. As long as they are alive, they exchange carbon with the atmosphere, keeping their internal ratio of carbon-14 to stable carbon constant. At death, the exchange ceases and the decay rate of carbon-14 begins to change the ratio. By measuring the carbon-14 ratio, scientists can determine how long ago death occurred.

Since the development of the process in the Mid-Twentieth Century AD it has been constantly fine-tuned. Counts of carbon-14 are now done with mass spectrometers. Calibration curves have been derived to account for known changes in the carbon isotope ratio over time. Adjustments have been developed to account for special cases. For example, humans absorb carbon through the food chain. A diet high in fish will bias the findings for human samples, indicating an earlier date than when death actually occurred.

Two irreducible imperfections remain. In mathematical terms, half life is an exponential function. Ignoring theory and restricting ourselves to practical terms, this means that while the remaining carbon-14 value can never reach zero, it can approach zero very closely. At some point the remaining carbon-14 value is too small to count. This limit is currently taken to be 50,000 years. The second imperfection is that precision is limited to a date range at a specific level of confidence. We will visit the concept of confidence level in a later chapter. Overall, the shortcomings of the methodology are minimal. Radiocarbon dating remains one of the most accurate and reliable tools available for establishing the age of artifacts.

The process was applied to dating the Santorini eruption when an olive branch was found just beneath the lava flow. The date of the death of the branch, therefore, was the date of the eruption. The date derived was 1627 BC to 1600 BC, with a 95% confidence level.

Archaeologists, using dating methods we will discuss later in the chapter, immediately challenged this date as too early. It did not conform to evidence that placed the date between 1570 BC and 1500 BC. The primary basis of challenge was the possibility of a slight deficiency in carbon-14 at the time of the eruption. This would result in a smaller ratio of carbon-14 in the sample and bias the findings toward an earlier date.

The idea of deficiency in carbon-14 does have foundation in fact. The packets of cosmic energy that create carbon-14 are emitted by the sun. Solar activity, and the resulting energy emissions, fluctuate over time. The calibration curve that accounts for variations in carbon-14 is built from data points comparing radiocarbon derived dates with known dates from other sources. As more data points become available, the curve becomes more precise. A recent upgrade brought the count of data points for the 1700 BC to 1500 BC period to around eight hundred. The resulting recalibration suggests a late Seventeenth BC date is the most likely candidate for the Santorini eruption. This corresponds with the original finding of 1627 BC to 1600 BC.

Dendrochronology

Dendrochronology is the measurement of time by counting annular tree rings. Trees grow at different rates in different years, depending on available moisture and other factors. When the tree is cut down and examined end-on, a pattern of rings of different thickness can be seen. Many trees in the temperate zones produce a growth ring every year. A count of these rings gives the age of the tree in years at the time it was felled and growth stopped.

The reading of tree rings is a complex undertaking. Alternating climate conditions in a single year can produce multiple rings. Other years may have missing rings. In some species, oak and elm for example, missing rings are rare. These are often selected to develop long term chronologies. A key factor in developing these chronologies, or tree ring histories, is the tendency of similar species in the same region to develop similar ring patterns. This allows scientists to work backwards, measuring rings in successive generations of trees where the patterns overlap.

Different types of chronologies can be developed. A floating chronology is one in which neither the beginning nor the end date is known. Such a chronology can be anchored to a specified set of dates by cross-matching to a chronology where dates are known. Anchored and fully cross-matched chronologies exist for oak and pine in central Europe going back more than 12,000 years, for oak in England and Ireland about 7,000 years and for bristlecone pine in California more than 8,000 years. Methods of reading tree rings have grown increasingly sophisticated. Technicians now employ computer algorithms involving statistical analysis.

An additional benefit of dendrochronology is that it gives clues as to weather conditions at various times during the tree's life. Thinner rings indicate less favorable growing conditions. In the case of the Santorini eruption, this can provide an indicator of volcanic winter.

Tree ring data indicate that a significant weather event interfered with growth in North America in the 1629-1628 BC period, plus or minus 65 years. A date of 1628 BC was derived from oak in Ireland and pine in Sweden. A date of 1627 BC was determined from frost rings in bristlecone pine. Later radiocarbon data from oak and bristlecone pines has suggested a revision of these dates to between 1600 BC and 1525 BC. The revision is itself subject to question based on limited knowledge of the original carbon-14 ratio.

Several difficulties exist in pinning down the date of the Santorini eruption using tree ring data. The presence of a volcanic winter is not the only factor that may have impacted tree ring growth. Weather is complex. Other factors may have been involved. There is no way to directly trace tree ring growth to the Santorini eruption. Tree ring history is also subject to re-calibration. Dendrochronology is only one element of the dating process.

An additional cautionary note is in order when it comes to establishing the date of volcanic winter. Scientists have conducted numerous studies to identify changes in climate over time. These are not useful for our purposes. Volcanic winter is a weather event. Weather is not climate. Weather events are transitory. Changes in climate may manifest themselves over centuries.

Stratigraphy

Volcanic eruptions are prime candidates for dating by stratigraphy. The general theory recognizes that both geologic events and civilizations build on top of one another over time, resulting in discrete layers. These layers are referred to as strata. If one item found in a layer can be dated, then all items in the layer are effectively dated. The layer of residue associated with the Santorini eruption is identifiable by its chemical fingerprint.

Dating by stratigraphy requires that the layers remain in the configuration in which they were originally laid down. Any disruption in the strata, for example by earthquake or human intervention, invalidates the dating. More subtle changes in ground structure can also occur over time, and can be equally disruptive.

This has created at least one area of confrontation in dating the Santorini eruption. Ejecta from the eruption were found during excavation of the ancient Nile Delta city of Avaris, at a layer dated to 1540 BC. It is not clear that this layer maintained its integrity over time. Nile Delta cities have been subjected to numerous disruptions. For example, the Bronze Age capitol of Pi-Ramses was found to have been moved stone by stone to a new location when the Nile silted at its original site.

The break between native soil and the residue of the eruption is clear on Santorini, where the Minoan city of Akrotiri was entombed largely intact. Dating the break is another matter. Radiocarbon results have already been discussed. Archaeologists have derived different results by examining artifacts found during the excavation of Akrotiri. This brings us to the intriguing and sometimes slippery discipline of pottery dating.

Seriation

Pottery has been a constant of civilization since it was first manufactured. It is made from readily available materials. It can be shaped to provide leak proof storage for valuable liquids and clean surfaces from which to consume meals. It is easily broken, but it will not deteriorate with time. An archaeologist can be reasonably sure of recovering a sizeable number of bits and pieces from any viable dig site. Modern computer algorithms can interpolate from the curves of a few remaining pieces and construct a virtual picture of an entire vessel broken thousands of years ago. In some cases traces of the pigment applied for decoration can be used to reconstruct the original design.

The pieces and reconstructions can provide date information due to civilization's fascination with style. In general changes in the style of the artifacts of life, pottery included, are serial in nature. A change will begin to assert itself in small numbers when it first appears, then grow to peak volume and gradually taper away in popularity as a new style comes into favor.

Pottery style is not limited to function, shape and decoration. It can be differentiated based on the mixture of clay used, whether it was made by hand or on a wheel, variations in wheel speed, whether it was fired under conditions of oxidation or reduction and chemical analysis of the pigments applied. Once a style has been reliably dated, every piece in that style can be assigned the same date range, no matter where it is found. The dating can be refined by the proportion of that style relative to earlier or later styles.

Datable pottery fragments have been found at numerous sites associated with the Santorini eruption, including the entombed city of Akrotiri. Fragments of gypsum pottery were found that are thought to originate from Syria in an era referred to by modern scholars as Middle Bronze Age II. The most recent (closest to modern) subcategory for this classification (Middle Bronze Age II C) aligns with dates from 1650 BC to 1550 BC in the Near East.

Pottery dating is not without problems. It is necessarily imprecise. A pottery style may have persisted for decades or even centuries. In addition, we have recovered only a minuscule fraction of all the pottery ever made.

We are guessing from a sample that may be statistically insignificant when a given style came into being and when it went out of fashion. A separate problem is that pottery dating is referential in nature. The date of any style of pottery is determined by reference to the layers in which it is found. That implies that the layer or layers have been dated by other means. The dating of the pottery is dependent on the accuracy and precision of those means.

For the purpose of dating the Santorini eruption pottery, upon which archaeologists have relied heavily, can be used to establish a rough framework. It can corroborate other results. It is not by itself capable of producing a precise result or overturning a result produced by other methods.

Documentation

Since the Santorini eruption took place during historical times, defined as times for which written records exist, we may be able to locate documents that provide or suggest a date for the eruption. An immediately obvious issue is that documents from this period are either undated or bear dates based on arcane calendars that must somehow be reconciled to our current concept of years before the birth of Christ.

Appropriate date ranges are normally assigned to undated documents according to two factors, content and context. In some cases, both tests can be applied. Dating by content involves inspection of the text of the document for reference to persons or events whose dates are known from other sources. Dating by context involves reference to a date already assigned to the site where the document was located. Depending on the medium on which the writing was done, radiocarbon dating may also be applied.

Establishing the dates of Near Eastern events in the period we are examining relies heavily on an Egyptian document called the *Turin King List*, thought to date from the Thirteenth Century BC reign of Pharaoh Ramses II, and on a list of dynasties compiled by the Egyptian historian Manetho in the Third Century BC. Both lists provide the names of Pharaohs and the years of their reign. By working backward from a known point, historians can establish a date range for any ruler. The process is complicated by the fact that the *Turin King List*, which we will consider in detail in a later chapter, exists only as fragments. No complete copy of Manetho's original work exists.

An example of the application of dating to the Bronze Age in general is the process used by Biblical scholars to establish the date for the ascension of King David. Biblical text says that David was followed by Solomon. Five years after the death of Solomon, Jerusalem was sacked by an Egyptian Pharaoh. Egyptian records establish that the sack occurred in 925 BC. This would place the death of Solomon at 930 BC. Estimating Solomon's reign at 40 years, David's death would have occurred in 970 BC, and his ascension approximately 30 years earlier, or 1000 BC.

Any reasonable person would question the wisdom of basing key historical dates on fragments of old writing. The need to validate the Egyptian chronology takes us to the city of Ugarit, an ancient port on the East coast of the Mediterranean. Ugarit was besieged and sacked, probably by the same Mycenaean expeditionary force that leveled Troy in Homer's *Iliad*. After the fall of Ugarit, the expeditionary force moved south into Egyptian controlled Canaan. In Homer's *Odyssey* Menelaus, the King of Sparta, boasts that he took treasure from foreign speaking people in the Egyptian lands. The expedition culminated in an attempt to conquer Egypt. The Egyptian chronology on which we rely for our dates says they were defeated by Pharaoh Ramses III in 1178 BC.

Ugarit is important because the city was never reclaimed after it fell. A trove of documents remained in situ. One tablet mentions a solar eclipse. It was, of course, inscribed before the city fell. Solar eclipses are regular occurrences that can be calculated to the day and hour. The arc of visibility can be accurately reckoned. An eclipse was visible in Ugarit in on January 21, 1192 BC. Ugarit must have fallen after that date, probably after 1184 BC. Allowing additional time for the plunder of Canaan, the Mycenaean expeditionary force would have reached Egypt around 1178 BC, corroborating the Egyptian chronology. Any difference would be classified as imprecision rather than error.

Once a date within the chronology can be anchored to an event whose timing is known, the chronology can be aligned with modern calendar dates. In the case of the Egyptian chronology, we are told by an Egyptian document known as the *Harris Papyrus* that one element of the defeated

Mycenaean force, called the Peleset, was resettled in Canaan. These were the Philistines, who bedeviled local rulers during the Biblical book of *Judges*. This allowed Biblical scholars to reasonably date the events of *Judges* and cross check the subsequent rise of kingship, first under Saul and then David. Without the anchor point of a solar eclipse, the entire scheme would be a historical house of cards.

Dating the Eruption

The concept of anchoring is one reason accurate dating of the Santorini eruption is important. It has the potential to provide an anchor point for the chronology of the period, either validating what we currently believe or forcing us to re-evaluate our conclusions and revise prevailing time lines.

The available evidence seems to suggest date around 1600 BC for the Santorini eruption. We will set 1600 BC as a preliminary estimate. The next step will be to look at additional indicators to either validate or revise that provisional date.

Before we delve into the details of when and how the Santorini eruption re-wrote history, we need to understand what the civilizations of the time world looked like.

THE WORLD OF BRONZE

At the time of the Santorini eruption bronze was the hallmark of the civilized world. The bronze of the era was an alloy of about 90% copper and 10% tin. The tin content varied according to whether hard weapons grade bronze or more malleable decorative bronze was required. A civilization is said to belong to the Bronze Age if it used bronze, regardless of whether it smelted the raw ores and alloyed the metal, imported the smelted components by commercial means and alloyed the metal or simply imported the alloyed metal, either as ingots or as finished goods.

Importation in some form was generally required. Copper ore (malachite) and tin ore (usually cassiterite) seldom occur in proximity to one another. Tin is disproportionately rare. In the absence of tin, arsenic was occasionally used as a substitute. The results were inferior. In the Near East, where the Bronze Age got off to an early start, copper was readily available. Tin was difficult to obtain. By the time of the Santorini eruption, the available sources were the Afghanistan-Uzbekistan-Tajikistan region, Central Europe, the Iberian Peninsula, the Brittany region of France and Cornwall in Britain. If there was going to be a long lasting Bronze Age, long range trade had to be established and maintained.

Trade is probably as old as civilization. Archaeologists have identified trade between population centers that existed well back into the Stone Age.

This grew gradually into a network of traceable land routes. Augmentation by riverine and seagoing transport is at least as old as the Egyptian pyramids.

By 1600 BC the network included long distance sea voyages. The western coast of India, for example, was accessible from Arabia as a result of geography and its impact on weather. During the hot months, the large land mass of the Himalaya Mountains warmed and drove winds in one direction. During cooler times, the Indian Ocean was warmer than the adjoining land and the winds reversed. This allowed sailing crews to make the voyage downwind in one direction, unload cargos, careen their vessels for maintenance and then load with locally procured cargo when the winds turned in favor of a return voyage. Excavation at the Indian port of Lothal shows activity as early as 2500 BC.

The absence of landmarks makes open sea navigation challenging. Latitude can be readily determined by observing the angle of the sun or the North Star. Accurate estimation of longitude requires the use of precise star charts. That called for a high level of astronomical and mathematical sophistication on the part of the civilizations participating in Bronze Age seagoing commerce.

The Minoans were heavily involved in maritime trade. Centrally located islands, including Santorini, gave them ready access to a large number of lucrative ports of call along the Aegean and Mediterranean coasts. How far they might have ventured beyond the Mediterranean is not known. Bronze Age anchors have been found in shallow harbors beyond the Strait of Gibraltar.

It requires a stretch of the imagination, but from Gibraltar it is theoretically possible to reach the Americas. The rotation of the Earth creates a clockwise current in the North Atlantic that flows from North Africa to the Bermuda area and then turns north as the Gulf Stream until it reaches Nova Scotia where it turns again, flowing to Scotland and thence south along the west coast of Europe. Sailing this route with the maritime technology of the Bronze Age would have been an immensely risky undertaking.

The other potential route from Europe to America lay in the north, via Iceland and Greenland. The route was used before Columbus. A Viking colony dated to about 1000 AD has been excavated in the Canadian province of Newfoundland. No European settlements have been found that could establish travel to America at or before 1600 BC.

While fragmentary indications have been interpreted to suggest such voyages may have been made, the idea is more intriguing than compelling. There is currently no available evidence of large scale trade between the Americas and the rest of the world at the time of the Santorini eruption.

Absent the Americas, the world of 1600 BC was largely interconnected. The Middle East lay at one focus of this interconnection. Some 700 years earlier the Akkadian empire controlled the Tigris and Euphrates valleys, parts of Canaan, the western part of modern Iran and southern part of modern Turkey. The empire had since broken into smaller spheres of influence, but the commercial network underlying it had survived. The universal trade language of the region in 1600 BC was still Akkadian, rendered in cuneiform. It transcended spheres of influence that had risen on tribal or geographic bases and enabled diplomacy as well as commerce.

A catastrophe that struck this region would reverberate through the interconnected world. That would magnify the impact beyond the scope of initial event or its physical aftermath. In order to appreciate the implications, we will need a summary understanding of the individual elements of the world of 1600 BC.

Asian Eastern Mediterranean

Asia bordering the Eastern Mediterranean consists of the Asian portion of modern Turkey, plus all of modern Syria, Lebanon, Israel and Palestine. In the last stage of the Middle Bronze Age, the area was sub-divided differently. The fertile Anatolian plateau of what is now Turkey was carved into several kingdoms. Powerful city-states controlled key points along inland trade routes and on the coast. No single ruler was able to gain hegemony. To the east, in the rugged Taurus Mountains, lurked the opportunistic Hittites. Between the Hittites and the Black Sea was the land of the Kaska, who bedeviled the Hittites for centuries, as the Hittites raided and bedeviled the kingdom of Aleppo and its vassal states in what is now Syria. Along the Mediterranean coast of what is now Lebanon, Israel and Palestine lay the land of Canaan, the home of traders, herders and farmers.

The Euphrates River, one of the world's longest, wound through the region, bringing fertility to the land, an efficient route for commerce and water to support urban centers. Crops grown and animals raised supported a large population, freeing many from the land to engage in specialized trades and mercantile ventures. An intricate network of caravan routes brought goods from areas farther inland to the Mediterranean and Aegean ports for distribution to distant lands. Ships brought imports for the caravans to take back to their lands of origin. Commerce provided the wealth to support the military and political power that protected the farmers, crafts people and merchants. It was a delicate balance. Any upset could have serious consequences.

Mediterranean Europe

Modern Mediterranean Europe consists of Greece and the nearby islands, the Balkan States, Italy, Southern France, Spain and Sardinia. We are limited in our understanding of the subdivisions existing around 1600 BC. Relevant contemporary writing comes from other cultures. Archeological work provides only physical evidence. Minoan cities were well established. Monumental architecture is present on Sardinia, although its purpose is unclear. Distribution of artifacts shows robust trade throughout the region. Later writing suggests that river commerce and overland portage provided linkage with cultures to the north.

The only culture we have much knowledge of is the Mycenaeans of mainland Greece. Burials suggest social stratification with a warrior class at the top. Political organization was along the lines of city-states. Trade goods of Mycenaean origin have been found as far away as Scotland. Isotopic analysis of some samples of Aegean bronze indicates that the tin was imported from Britain. Later writing speaks of ongoing conflict with mountain tribes, suggesting the Mycenaeans had a somewhat tenuous hold on their lands.

Archaeological finds suggest a connection between the Mycenaeans and the Minoans prior to the Santorini eruption. This may have been a mercenary arrangement. According to later historical writing the Minoan commercial complex was under constant threat from piracy. That is probably true. Piracy had been a long standing issue in Mediterranean trade, as evidenced by early writing from the region.

Mediterranean Africa

The primary divisions of Mediterranean Africa in the last stages of the Middle Bronze Age were Egypt and Libya.

At the time, Libya was not the country we know today. The name referred to as much of non-Egyptian Africa as was known then. It shared a border with Egypt and its rulers coveted the fertile land of the Nile Delta. The border was a point of military contention throughout the coexistence of the two powers.

Egypt at the time of the Santorini eruption was a nation divided. The traditional Pharaoh ruled the southern portion from the city of Thebes. The northern portion, primarily the Nile Delta, was ruled by a people called the Hyksos whose capitol was the city of Avaris. Who the Hyksos were and how they came to power has long been a matter of speculation and debate.

There is no speculation about the importance of Egypt. It was the bread basket of the Eastern Mediterranean. Regular flooding of the Nile River provided long term arable land to produce staple crops for home consumption and export. Trade goods, many of them luxury items, arrived from as far away as India. In terms of self sufficiency, Egypt was the most stable economy of the time.

Stability had nurtured centuries of cultural development. The Egyptian system of hieroglyphic writing was among the earliest devised. Surviving documents attest to a high level of mathematical and medical sophistication. Its most enduring engineering achievement, the pyramids at Giza, had already been in existence for more than eight hundred years at the time of the Santorini eruption. Egypt was connected commercially to the Asiatic Eastern Mediterranean by both seaports and by the Horus Road. What impacted one region could easily spill over into the other.

Mesopotamia

Sometimes referred to as the Fertile Crescent or the cradle of civilization, Mesopotamia was the land generally defined by the Tigris and Euphrates Rivers. The Fertile Crescent is the portion (including parts of Syria and

Turkey) lying in the shadow of the Taurus and Zagros Mountains, where seasonal rainfall was plentiful.

Sumerian civilization grew in the arid southern portions, where only the rivers provided water. The civilization was characterized by written communication and civil administration organized into city-states. Comprehensive irrigation systems supported intensive agriculture. The advent of a drier climate in the Third Millennium BC brought a series of wars between the city-states for control of arable land.

An outgrowth of those conflicts was the establishment of a professional military. A standing army enabled the creation of the Akkadian Empire. The Empire built an extensive road network and postal system to facilitate administration, and imposed its language for commercial and diplomatic purposes over wide areas of the Near East. The Akkadian Empire disintegrated within two centuries, but the infrastructure remained.

Following the disintegration of the Akkadian Empire a succession of kings at the city-state level claimed to control the region. None were able to impose their will as widely as the imperial rulers. Around 1800 BC the city of Babylon arose as pre-eminent. In its time it was a center of mathematics and astronomy, famed for its wealth and architecture. Its power was growing tenuous by the time of the Santorini eruption. It was under threat from the Kassites of western Iran.

Britain

Britain was a world away from cosmopolitan Mesopotamia in both distance and sophistication. It is worth a separate glance because we have a time capsule from the period. A village in the fenlands of south England, built over water on stilts, was destroyed in a fire. Bowls with food still in them indicate that the residents were surprised and forced to flee. The village fell into the marsh and the fire was extinguished. The residents made no attempt at salvage. The village was preserved in the anoxic environment of the silt beneath, providing a snapshot of life as it was lived at the moment the fire began. We can reasonably extrapolate the findings across Europe because the partial remains of similar villages have been found there.

The British site is dated to about 1000 BC, somewhat later than the Santorini eruption. Several dugout log boats were found in the proximity, some dating back to 1750 BC, and some closer to the date of the destruction of the site. That suggests that the mode of living in the region did not change significantly in the intervening years.

The settlement was about the size of a small American farming community from the early Twentieth Century AD. It differed in that it was built inside a defensive palisade. There were individual structures that would have housed either a single or an extended family. A solid wheel suitable for a cart or wagon was found. Fabric fragments establish that weaving and garment making was practiced. Evidence of long distance trade appeared in the form of glass beads from Italy. Glass was rare and highly prized at the time, even in urban cultures. If the settlement was trading for luxury goods, they would have had a surplus of at least one commodity, probably textiles or food.

The site was part of Britain's Wessex culture. Although it was responsible for the final phase of construction of Stonehenge (1930 BC – 1600 BC), Wessex was a Bronze Age culture. Britain was one of the few areas where copper and tin ores coexisted in quantity within reasonable distances of one another. Tin was available from Devon and Cornwall and copper from the Great Orme Mine in North Wales. Tin was widely exported. Copper was alloyed with both tin to make bronze and zinc to make brass. Archaeologists have yet to locate actual metalworking sites dating from before about 1200 BC; however it is likely they existed in quantity.

Central and Northern Europe

Bronze Age cultures in Central Europe were not only similar to those in Britain; they were connected to them by traceable commerce. Perhaps the best known Bronze Age artifact from Europe is the *Nebra Sky Disk*, a metal plate representing portions of the night sky. Isotopic analysis shows the tin content of bronze used to make the plate came from Cornwall in England. Gold used in the decoration also originated in England.

Prominent on the disc are a cluster of stars thought to represent the constellation Pleiades. The constellation was important to European agriculture. The Pleiades disappear from the European sky in March, just when crops need to be planted. It is a celestial event that occurs predictably, regardless of the vagaries of local weather. That suggests celestial observation was used for more than ritual.

The plate was a product of the Unetice Culture, prevalent in Central Europe until about 1600 BC. A few rich burials support the idea of social stratification. Wide distribution of Unetice artifact testifies to extensive commerce.

The Bronze Age in Northern Europe arose late (around 1700 BC), mainly as a result of trade with cultures that produced bronze objects. Rock carvings depicting boats suggest that waterborne commerce played an important role. The absence of written records requires us to date the carvings by comparison with the items depicted. Some appear to go back to the Stone Age, allowing speculation that the ships were available for use at the beginning of the bronze trade. Overland routes also existed. Those carried amber from the Baltic region to the Mediterranean.

Central Asia

Central Asia is the source of a much-debated theory of Bronze Age migration. In its initial form, called the Seima-Turbino Phenomenon, it had cultures spreading west and east from the Altai Mountain range in what is now Southern Russia and Mongolia in the hundred or so years on either side of 2000 BC. Bronze made with tin from the Altai Mountains has been found as far west as Moldova. Caucasian mummies have been found in the Far East. That evidence falls short of supporting a migration theory. It does suggest that Central Asia provided overland contact between East and West. Cultures and languages in the two areas remained notably independent.

Recent genetic studies establish that the main migration from the east into Europe began around 3000 BC. Contact between the two areas was in place long before 2000 BC.

The central location of modern day Iran gave cultures arising there control over the caravan routes that provided the backbone of overland trade through the region. This was the Biblical land of Elam. It was centered at Anshan on the Iranian Plateau in the earlier part of the Middle Bronze age, and at Susa in modern Kazakhstan in the later stages. The economy was mainly supported by agriculture, and featured advanced water management techniques. Writing from the region remains obscure.

South Asia

Urban civilization arose in South Asia in the Indus River Valley of what is now Pakistan, first at Mohenjo Daro and then at Harrapa. The cultures of both cities were literate, but we are unable to translate the symbols they used. The Harrapan culture vanished around 1800 BC. The center of South Asian civilization moved to the Ganges River Valley in India. Rather than occupying large urban areas, the population spread among numerous fortified towns.

Independent fiefdoms ranged down the West coast of the Indian sub-continent, providing ports of call for the maritime trade from the Arabian Peninsula. Based upon artifacts discovered on the sub-continent and throughout the Middle East, commerce had grown robust by 1600 BC. Large scale rice cultivation suggests an influx of population and agricultural technology from China.

Overland trade was probably limited by the towering mountains of Afghanistan. DNA evidence and archaeological finds establish that migration and technology transfer did occur. The mountains were a difficulty rather than an insurmountable obstacle.

China

The Bronze Age in China began around 2000 BC. There is disagreement as to whether importation of western technology or independent discovery was involved. Chinese bronze tends to have a higher tin content, making for a harder and more brittle metal. This may argue for separate development or simply represent a different approach to metal working.

The beginning of the Bronze Age was a transitional period for China. The prevailing Erlitou culture was moving from scattered town and village centers toward urbanization. The political climate of the times involved dynastic rule. The economy had its foundation in organized agriculture and animal husbandry. It was reliant to a significant degree on major rivers.

The two great rivers of China, the Yellow and the Yangtze, offered permanent arable land only if the floods and flow could be controlled. These present formidable engineering challenges even today. We have only limited insight into the prehistoric cultures that first successfully addressed the issues. The books that might have contained details were burned in ancient times. It is clear, however, that the survival of the cultures depended on the resulting agricultural output. Any disruption could be catastrophic.

Overview

In 1600 BC an interconnected world faced multiple threats from the Santorini eruption. Some cultures could not escape direct physical damage. Only North America, which remained in the Stone Age and isolated by two great oceans, had any buffer against the loss of vital commerce. Civilizations beyond the reach of the eruption and the following volcanic winter could be overrun by populations fleeing famine.

Not all of the potential impacts were negative. Competition for scarce resources would favor societies that were better organized and more technically advanced. Less able players would be weeded out. Civilization would tend to consolidate along the most effective lines.

We will look most closely at those areas where we can identify the Santorini eruption as having its most profound impact. In some cases a legacy persisting to this day.

FAMINE IN CANAAN

We will begin our examination of the broader impact of the Santorini eruption in the land of Canaan. Canaan lay on the east coast of the Mediterranean, directly in the path of the stratospheric sulfate aerosol veil borne on the upper level winds. It was also the land of the Old Testament. Memory of the effects of volcanic winter, crop failure and obliteration of the graze required to support animal husbandry, became part of regional lore. That lore underlay the beginning chapters of Judeo-Christian scripture.

Biblical reference raises the question of how much is faith and how much is fact. Large scale archaeological efforts to establish the veracity of the Old Testament continue to this day. Before we address the factual basis of scripture, we should take a brief excursion into what archaeology is and what it isn't.

The word archaeology is a combination of two Greek words that translate roughly to *speaking of old things*. It began as a discipline in the 1760's AD when a librarian name Johann Winklemann undertook a systematic study of the then recently discovered cities of Pompeii and Herculaneum, buried in the 79 AD eruption of Mount Vesuvius. Many ancient cities were known before then. In some cases their ruins were visible above ground. Exploration had been limited to treasure hunts for decorative artifacts. No attempt had been made to understand the civilizations that built them.

In the following years archaeology grew into a discipline that recognized that the value of artifacts lay in the context in which they were found. It is not uncommon today to leave potentially productive areas unexcavated so the artifacts contained there can be recovered in context at a later time when the science available to analyze them has advanced beyond what is available today.

An example of the use of science and context is the chance find of a mass burial in the south of England. The grave contained only the skeletons of young males, all dead by violence, with no explanation of how they came to be there. Analysis of oxygen isotopes in their teeth established that they had matured in a colder northern climate. Radiocarbon dating placed them in the Viking era. This led to the likely conclusion that they were the survivors of a Viking raiding party shipwrecked in the nearby coastal waters. Their struggles to reach shore had left them exhausted and unarmed, easy prey for English warders who apprehended and executed them.

Science and context do not blend into a magic elixir. Possibly the best known example is an artifact called the *Antikythera Machine*. The artifact was brought up from a shipwreck in the Strait of Malaga, the treacherous forty miles of open water between the southernmost tip of mainland Greece and the island of Crete. A shipwreck is as close to perfect context as we can get. One of the artifacts recovered by salvors was a lump of fused metal that appeared to have once been some sort of mechanism. The wreck was tentatively dated to the first century AD, when no comparable mechanism was known to exist. In time science caught up with the mystery and the mechanism was determined to be a sophisticated astronomical model capable of representing even the complex cycles of the moon. We knew the what, where and when, but we still don't know how it was used; whether it was some treasure being transported to a wealthy buyer or part of the ship's standard navigation kit. Archaeology is often as good at raising questions as it is at answering them.

Context is not limited to physical location. An example is an Egyptian document called the *Rhind Mathematical Papyrus,* which will become important later in our examination. The writer of the document gives the regnal year and month of a known Egyptian ruler as the date of preparation. This allows us to place it in historical context regardless of where it was found. Unfortunately that sort of occurrence is rare.

In summary, archaeology is a hit and miss proposition that depends as much on blind luck as rigorous analysis for its success. It is hobbled by economic and political constraints, frustrated by local tomb raiders who scatter artifacts out of context and, except in special cases, limited to non-perishable finds. Tidbits of archaeological evidence may support historical narrative. Their absence does not invalidate it. For example, it is known that the conqueror Genghis Khan returned to his native Mongolia to be buried. His tomb remains undiscovered in spite of the considerable time, toil and treasure expended in the search. Similarly, the narrative of Judeo Christian scripture may have historical merit even without archaeological corroboration.

The Bible is as much an institution as a book. It was the first work printed after the development of moveable type. It is a perennial best seller in spite of the fact that copies are readily available free of charge. It would be difficult to find a language into which it has not been translated. It is widely quoted as the ultimate source of wisdom. It remains the subject of a long-standing labor of scholarship to figure out how it came into being and who compiled it. Before we take Biblical references at face value, we need to examine the history of the work to gain a sense of how reliable scripture is as a source of the history it claims to portray.

The need for a Bible arose from the aftermath of the conquest of Israel by the Babylonians in 586 BC. In the Biblical version, the Israelites were taken to Babylon as slaves. Written tablets from the period indicate many Israelites went voluntarily to pursue commercial or administrative opportunities in the premier urban center of the time. The two scenarios are not mutually exclusive. The true situation may have been a hybrid of both, with the framers of scripture choosing to emphasize the one that suited their purposes. There is no doubt that Babylon held a large community of expatriate Israelites.

In 537 BC Babylon was in turn conquered by the Persians. The Persians returned the descendants of the expatriate Israelites to their homeland in what amounted to forced repatriation. The reasons are debated. Some historians argue that the Persians wanted a buffer state between themselves and Egypt. It may be that the Persians simply wanted to purge their newly conquered city of a fractious and potentially subversive element that had insinuated its way into commerce and civil administration. Whatever the case, there was a significant displacement of population that demanded an immediate re-settlement effort.

For the descendants of ambitious Israelite migrants, now themselves successful urban merchants and administrators, being shipped out to the hinterlands to babysit flocks of sheep probably wasn't the next step in their career plans. The people who had remained in Israel during the Babylonian exile would have been even less happy. A large influx of newcomers meant hungry mouths to feed and additional competition for a finite set of resources. If the Jewish priesthood in Canaan were to maintain its power and influence, it has to unify the returnees and residents under a single god.

There was no shortage of sects and cults competing for followers. Choice of religion often determined how well people prospered, and even how well they ate. Sects focusing on animal sacrifice would cook the sacrificial animal for the congregation to feast on following the ceremony.

Evidence of how seriously the possibility of desertion by the faithful was taken can be found in the frequency of criticism of competing religions, from the Jewish denunciation of idolatry in *Genesis* to the epistles (letters) in *Revelation,* the final book of Christian text. The threat of apostasy was driven home in dramatic fashion by the story of Jezebel, a Ninth Century BC Tyrian princess who married into Israelite royalty and brought with her the pagan gods of her homeland. The story has her ordering the execution of Jewish priests and coming perilously close eradication of the Jewish religion before she is brought down by the power of God. Scholars disagree on whether she actually existed. Real or invented, the story underscores the fear of apostasy harbored by the framers of the Bible.

Returnees from Babylon would have compounded the problem. They would have been exposed to, and perhaps persuaded to worship, an amorphous deity called Marduk. In addition to pagan gods from Canaan, the priests faced another source of religious competition.

The Jewish priests' solution was to create a sense of shared history, religion and rules of law that their target congregation could identify with. The Bible was originally conceived as the permanent written work upon which this sense would be based and from which it could be communicated. In order to be broadly accepted, the contents of the work had to resonate with the entire audience. To ensure the widest possible acceptance, the priests crafted their work around stories that were already well known.

An example is the tale of Noah and the Flood. This tale first surfaces as part of the Sumerian *Epic of Gilgamesh,* dated to around 2700 BC. In Babylonian literature the story appears in the *Atrahasis Epic.* In Greek lore it turns up as the myth of Deucalion. The priests of Israel simply replaced the storm god of the Sumerians, the Earth god of the Babylonians and the Greek Pantheon with their own Yahweh (YHWH in the original vowelless Aramaic writing and Jehovah in modern parlance). Other details were re-worked to conform to the Jewish beliefs and experiences of the time. The geography was reset to Israel. Animals were selected based on religious doctrines of purity. The dimensions and description of the ark morphed from a Mesopotamian coracle design to something more familiar to Canaanite shipwrights.

An interesting note on the Bible story of the Flood is that it is in fact two stories, mutually contradictory in places, woven together in the same two pages. This suggests that the Bible was not intended to be read directly by the audience, sizable portions of which were probably illiterate, but rather read to them by priests. Different segments of the audience might have different beliefs. Individual priests could choose accordingly and read the acceptable version.

This brings us to the subject of the Santorini eruption. The ensuing volcanic winter would have resulted in a memorable famine. If there had been a famine in Canaan sufficiently catastrophic for its memory to persist through centuries, it would have made a promising core around which to build a Biblical epic. This appears to have been the case in the book of *Genesis.* Two of the major storylines involve famine in Canaan as primary plot motivation.

The first story we are concerned with begins in the Chaldean city of Ur, located on the southern portion of the Euphrates River. A patriarch named Terah, who is engaged in the manufacture of religious idols, is shown the error of his ways by his son Abram (later morphed into Abraham). Terah decides to abandon his lucrative but sinful business and take his family north along the Euphrates, where he settles in the city of Harran, near the southern border of modern Turkey. In the early portion of the Bible decisions are always made by patriarchs. The priests had a strong interest in maintaining the existing structure of patriarchal authority in society. If they could influence patriarchs, others would follow.

Upon the death of Terah, Abram became patriarch. God instructs Abram to move again, this time to a land God will show him. There he will make a great nation. Fast forward through a few adventures to the area of Nablus in Canaan, where Abram settles and builds an altar to God. Famine in Canaan forces Abram to travel to Egypt to find provisions for his family. It is important to note that it was not in the priests' interest to invent famine in Canaan. The idea calls into question the power of God. Why would God direct Abram into Canaan and then permit famine to drive him out? It is more likely that famine in Canaan was a real event, which the priests had to address in a forthright manner to maintain credibility.

According to the Bible, when Abram presented himself in Egypt the Pharaoh was besotted with Abram's wife, Sarah, and bestowed great wealth on the family. This can be dismissed. As professional preachers, the priests writing the story would have been acutely aware that the best way to lose an audience was to start sermonizing. They spiced their work with as many battles, besottings and begattings as they could cram in. An apocryphal (non-Biblical) text offers a spicier and more specific version of Sarah's physical beauty, probably developed for use by a particular sect.

The concept of famine in Canaan is less easily done away with. It returns with a vengeance when we get to the story of Abram's grandson, Joseph. Abram's son, Jacob has journeyed from Harran into Canaan and begotten a large family of shepherds. The audience for the Bible included a good number of shepherds. It was in the interest of the priests to make the protagonists shepherds. The youngest son, Joseph, is Jacob's favorite. Joseph's brothers, understandably chagrined, plot to do away with him. Eventually they wind up selling him to a group of slave traders who, in turn, sell Joseph into slavery in Egypt. Joseph rises to power in Egypt and is placed in charge of doling out provisions. Along comes famine in Canaan and Joseph's brothers are sent to Egypt with money to buy food.

The details of the story are invention for the convenience of the priesthood. For example, money did not come into use until just before 600 BC, when the first known coinage was made from electrum, an alloy of gold and silver. The point of the story appears to be reconciliation between a fortunate son risen to prosperity in a foreign land and the less fortunate left at home tending the sheep. The backdrop of famine in Canaan provides a familiar setting for the tale. The priests could not have gotten any mileage out of it unless there had been a catastrophic famine in Canaan that had persisted in oral and written lore.

The repeated use of famine in Canaan in *Genesis* could have had its origin with famine resulting from the Santorini eruption, but it is difficult to align the two. Establishing dates for early events in the Bible is an exercise in frustration. The normal approach to establishing historical dates is to count backward or forward from an anchored event, using the life spans given for the historical participants. The life spans given for the characters in *Genesis* are unrealistic. For example, Terah is cited as living 205 years, although in the Samaritan version he only makes it to 145.

It is unlikely that the priests composing the book of *Genesis* had knowledge of the exact dates of the events they were using to frame their stories. There was no reason for them to care. They just needed to approximate a chronology that met the credibility standards of an illiterate audience. Their goal was to use the common recollection of events to bind a disparate group together under their tutelage.

Another timing issue also comes into play. As with most ancient texts, we do not have the original version of the Old Testament. The fact that a book says Bible on the cover does not guarantee that it faithfully reproduces the writing of the original author(s). In the case of the Old Testament, the text was laboriously copied and re-copied by hand, letter for letter, for two thousand years, between the compilation of the early books in the decades before 500 BC to the development of moveable type printing in the century before 1500 AD. An interval of that length creates a significant potential for divergence from the original text.

In order to estimate the potential for copy errors, scholars compare the text of the oldest complete copy, which for the Old Testament dates to the Ninth Century AD, with portions of the same text found on older fragments. There is never one to one correspondence, but the fewer the differences, the more accurate the complete copy is judged to be. This begs the question of how legitimate the fragments are. The price of bits of antiquity can be quite high. For sought-after religious antiquities the figures can be astronomical. This is an invitation to fraud, which can be difficult to detect.

In the case of the Old Testament, we do have a valid comparison point in the *Dead Sea Scrolls*. The *Scrolls* emerged in the years following World War II as finds from caves in the Qumram area of what was then Palestine. The *Scrolls*, or fragments thereof, found their way from the Bedouin shepherds who recovered them into a network of dealers, who then maneuvered them onto the market. There is certainly some fabrication in the legend of how various individual scrolls found their way to public notice. This is largely connected with evasions of modern law, which are epidemic in the antiquities trade. The *Scrolls* themselves are genuine. Radiocarbon dating has placed various of them from the Second Century BC to the First Century AD.

Scholars spent decades deciphering and reconstructing them to the extent possible. The key find was a nearly complete rendition of the book of *Isaiah*. Preserved in the protection of a pottery jar and the dry climate of the desert, the *Scroll* was physically imposing as well as historically significant. It unrolled to twenty four feet long, its segments (pages for modern comparison) sewn together. It was radiocarbon dated to the Second Century BC, no more than four centuries after its original composition.

The text was a close match to the book of *Isaiah* contained in the Ninth Century AD copy of the complete Old Testament. That suggests a very low rate of copy error over the centuries. That in turn suggests that the Ninth Century AD copy was a faithful rendition of the original, and by extension that our version of the book of *Genesis* is very close to what the priests originally wrote.

Surviving portions of *Genesis* in the *Dead Sea Scrolls* are fragmentary, but they do tally with modern scripture. Additional recovery of *Scroll* text may be possible. A project is underway to sequence the DNA of sheepskin and cowhide used as media. A matching of bits of media may allow matching of currently random fragments of text.

It is fair to ask what difference all that makes. Biblical stories, however faithful modern copies may be to the original, were set down more than a thousand years after the Santorini eruption. If we can't align Biblical tales of famine in Canaan with the date of the Santorini eruption, what good do they do us? Fortunately the old priests' choice of stories provides an attractive avenue of exploration. In both narratives, famine in Canaan drove the Israelites into Egypt in search of food. Contemporary Egyptian writing from the time of the Santorini eruption has survived. We have inscriptions on stone monuments and fragments of papyrus preserved by the arid desert climate.

The patriarch Jacob settled his family in the land of Goshen, identified by scholars as lying between the eastern edge of the Nile Delta and the Bitter Lakes region. If the Biblical tale does represent a sizeable influx of people from Canaan into Egypt, then there should be some mention in the Egyptian records. Egyptian documents from the period can often be assigned dates. That will allow alignment of the recorded events with the Santorini Eruption.

EGYPT I: RISE OF
THE FOREIGNERS

To gain an appreciation of the state of affairs in Egypt in the last stage of the Middle Bronze Age we need to go back to the beginning of Egypt as a nation. The country was built around the agricultural wealth created by the Nile River. Each year the River flooded and left rich soil on its banks when the floods receded. Around 3100 BC an enterprising ruler known today as Narmer brought the country together into a single unit. The resulting nation stretched from the coast, where the Nile Delta emptied into the Mediterranean Sea, southward to the second cataract of the River.

In the following centuries Egypt grew more sophisticated. The nation was organized into forty two administrative districts called nomes, each roughly equivalent to an American county. These were overseen by local officials who were overseen in turn by a vizier who reported to the Pharaoh. The Pharaoh was a living god and the supreme religious, military and political authority who ruled over every aspect of national life. With the Nile providing a uniform agricultural base and a ready avenue of communication, Egypt was naturally suited to function as a single unit. National wealth coupled with unity of government and purpose enabled such advances as the refinement of hieroglyphic writing and the development of the engineering skills necessary to build the great pyramids at Giza around 2500 BC.

Recent archaeological finds have given us a more accurate insight into the organization of the pyramid project. Ancient observers viewing the pyramids two thousand or more years after their construction imagined that vast armies of slaves had been required to construct the monuments. Excavation of the living quarters of the pyramid builders has revealed a population of skilled crafts people who saw themselves as elite and were honored to have been chosen to participate in such an important public work. They were probably a select part of the large labor pool that came available to the Pharaoh at the completion of harvest and the beginning of the annual Nile floods. The massive blocks from which the pyramids were constructed were not dragged over long distances by forced labor. Papyrus pieced together from finds at the port of Wadi al Jarf indicate that the blocks were floated close to the building site by channeling the floods of the Nile. The picture of Egypt that emerges, both then and in the following centuries, is one of a unified, technologically capable society with a strong sense of national integrity and pride.

Archaeology can take us only so far in reconstructing a comprehensive picture of Egypt as it once was. As impressive as the archaeological finds of the last two centuries have been, they represent a tiny fraction of all that once existed in the distant past. We are fortunate to have a written legacy, but again that can take us only so far. Contemporary writing survives as tantalizing fragments that lend themselves to multiple and often conflicting interpretations. This leaves us reliant to a large degree on histories created in ancient times, by researchers who had access to documents and lore now lost.

The earliest history we have is carved on a monument called the *Palermo Stone*, thought to date from around 2400 BC. Additional work in the form of lists of kings (mostly Pharaohs) appears to have been composed in the Thirteenth Century BC. The only comprehensive history known to have been compiled in ancient times is a document called the *Aegyptica*. It was written by a priest/historian named Manetho, probably in the Second Century BC. This work was compiled under the patronage of a later Greek Pharaoh, possibly Ptolemy II.

The Ptolemies were a foreign dynasty. They came to power as a result of the conquest of Egypt by Alexander the Great and fell three centuries later with the Roman conquest and subsequent death of the last queen, Cleopatra. Alexander commissioned the building of a city named Alexandria in his honor. The city prospered under royal patronage. In time it became home to the premier library of the ancient world. The catalog of historical material available in the time of Manetho is not known. Based upon what we know of the scope and detail of his writing it must have been substantial.

Access to extensive source material does not guarantee an unbiased account. While the Ptolemiea were undoubtedly interested in learning the history of Egypt, they also had an interest in slanting its presentation to suit their political agenda. How much influence this had in Manetho's preparation of the *Aegyptica* is not known. It may not matter. Bias does not diminish the historical value of facts contained in the work. It was Manetho who divided centuries of Egyptian rule into the system of dynasties still used by modern scholars. Unfortunately Manetho's *Aegyptica* survives as only about 75 fragments. Otherwise we are dependent upon references to it made by the First Century AD historian Flavius Josephus.

Josephus was a unique character uniquely positioned in history. He was born into Jewish nobility in 37 AD and educated in the history of Judaism. When the Jews revolted against Rome in 66 AD, Josephus' autobiography has him appointed military commander of Jewish forces in Galilee. By his account there were some 65,000 men under his command. Most deserted in the face of Roman advances. Josephus was captured. A deft manipulator, he managed to switch sides. His voluminous writings were sponsored by three successive Roman emperors, Vespasian, Titus and Diocletian.

There is the question of how faithful the surviving material is to the original. For example, Josephus cites the height of a certain mountain peak as 30 stadia (about 18,000 feet). The true height of the peak is 3 stadia. As to whether this is exaggeration by Josephus or an indication that later copyists were error prone or given to revision we can only speculate. His works became the only source of information about many facets of the early days of Christianity. They survived while other sources deteriorated into fragments or vanished entirely because it served the Christian Church to preserve them.

Josephus is known to have spent time in Alexandria. Based on his writings he had access to the text of Manetho's work. He may have been working from a copy of the *Aegyptica* several generations removed from the original. Josephus' reiteration of Manetho, some of which he claims to be verbatim, is contained in a work called *Against Apion*. The work is a critique of anyone and everyone who did not credit Jewish culture with all that Josephus believed it deserved. While *Against Apion* comes to us intact, the references to Manetho are fragmentary and selected to support Josephus' theme. Some of the content is questionable. At one point Josephus tells us that Homer did not write his poems, but simply preserved them in song for others to copy down later. Josephus needs to be read with skepticism.

From the work of ancient historians and the fragments of contemporary writing unearthed by archaeologists we will piece together the best picture we can of Egypt as it was at the time of the Santorini eruption. Glyphs from the reign of Pharaoh Senusret, around 1900 BC, show a group of Asiatics entering Egypt, apparently with the blessing of the Pharaoh. These may be the people referred to as the Hyksos, who had established themselves in the Nile Delta by around 1800 BC. In Egyptian the Hyksos were called *heqa khasewet*. This name has been variously transliterated as *foreign rulers, rulers of foreigners* or *rulers of foreign lands*. The last is currently preferred by most scholars. The name had appeared in previous contexts referring to various chieftains in Nubia, Syria and Palestine. Josephus maintained that this particular group consisted of the children of the Biblical Jacob who had taken up residence in Egypt to escape famine in Canaan.

Many scholars tend toward the idea that the Hyksos were a multi-ethnic group that gravitated to the Nile Delta as professionals, trades people, craftsmen, merchants and laborers, possibly with a few mercenaries and bandits thrown in. Tending to contradict this is a Stela from the reign of a contemporary Pharaoh, which refers to the then current ruler of the Hyksos as a Canaanite chief. The two ideas are not mutually exclusive. It is possible that a Canaanite ruled over a multi-ethnic population.

A foreign presence in Egypt, particularly in the Nile Delta, which lay closest to Asia, comes as no surprise. Egypt was agriculture rich and resource poor. They exported great quantities of grain and beer in return for raw materials such as copper and tin to make bronze and timber from Canaan. Also imported were supplementary comestibles and finished goods in the form of gemstones, perfumes, textiles, even the natron and spices necessary for mummification. It is likely the Hyksos gained a foothold in the Nile Delta at least in part as expediters of this commerce.

Competing theories of the origin of the Hyksos do exist. One has the Pharaoh Amenemhat III importing a large group of Asiatics as labor for the extensive public works undertaken during his rule. This would be contradictory to indications of public works being used to occupy the labor of the large group of native Egyptian farmers displaced annually by the Nile floods. Another theory has the Hyksos invading Egypt en mass and seizing control of the Delta with chariots, superior weapons and armor. Manetho has them burning the city of Memphis on their way to the conquest of Northern Egypt. Archaeological excavation has uncovered no signs of contemporary destruction at Memphis. No signs of chariot factories or repair facilities were found during excavation of the Hyksos' capital of Avaris.

The invasion theory has another problem. There is no reason the Hyksos would stop at the Delta. It would be to their advantage to use their allegedly superior military technology to overrun the entire country and thus remove any potential threat to their rule.

A more likely scenario arises from a history of shifting power in Egypt. In theory the Pharaoh was all-powerful. In practice the administrators of individual nomes wielded considerable influence in their own domains. Weakness in the central government in Thebes was often exploited by local administrators to enhance their own positions. It is thought that the Theban government became too weak to prevent the rise of small autonomous fiefdoms in the Delta. No later than 1700 BC these fiefdoms were consolidated into Hyksos control of the Nile Delta region of Egypt.

This control was firmly in place by the rule of traditional Pharaoh Sequenenre Tao II. There were harsh diplomatic exchanges between the Pharaoh and the Hyksos king. The mummy of Sequenenre Tao II shows that he died of sharp force trauma, possibly but not necessarily in battle with the Hyksos. The Hyksos kings were not able to enforce their will in Southern Egypt, which continued to be ruled from Thebes.

As a point of interest, the traditional rulers of Egypt did not use the title Pharaoh until the reign of Merneptah, just before 1200 BC. This detail is generally overlooked by scholars. All native Egyptian rulers are referred to as Pharaohs. We will continue this convention to help us discriminate between the traditional Theban rulers and the Hyksos kings.

The Hyksos rulers of Northern Egypt and the traditional Pharaohs of Southern Egypt came to a practical form of coexistence involving transit and pasturage. The situation produced ambivalence on the part of traditional Egyptian society. An illustration is found in *Carnarvon Tablet I,* a contemporary writing in which the advisors of the Pharaoh Kamose counseled against upsetting the status quo. The advisors pointed out that Southern Egypt was secure as far north as the city of Elephantine, at the first cataract of the Nile.

As the ruler of a once unified country, Kamose saw the Hyksos as a stain on the integrity of Egypt as a nation. As Pharaoh, Kamose prevailed. During his reign, thought to last only about three years, he launched raids against the Hyksos capitol of Avaris. He claimed victory, but in fact accomplished little. The Hyksos remained in firm control of the Delta. This was essentially the state of Egypt in the last stage of the Middle Bronze Age. A king (probably Canaanite) ruled the Nile Delta and might well have been a magnet for Canaanite refugees from famine. The book of *Genesis,* composed more than a thousand years later, might well have referred to any ruler in Egypt as Pharaoh, even though the term was not in use in the Middle Bronze Age.

A large influx of Asiatics was in fact reported in an Egyptian document called the *Ipuwer Papyrus.* The document survives only as a damaged copy. It appears to have originated in the Middle Bronze Age, based upon two indications. First, the vocabulary and syntax of the contents are typical of the time. Second, Ipuwer, the name of the author, was a name in common usage during the Middle Bronze Age. The surviving copy has been radiocarbon dated to no earlier than 1250 BC.

That presents a problem when it comes to dating the reported influx of Asiatics. It is, however, helpful in establishing the document as a bona fide report and not simply a piece of the propaganda common in Egypt or a prophecy without foundation in fact. Clearly the document is not reporting the events of 1250 BC. Egypt had expanded north and east into Asia more than two centuries earlier. The Pharaoh in 1250 BC was Ramses II, an aggressive leader and one of the most powerful ever to rule.

A quarter of a century earlier he had taken an army of five divisions north into Syria and fought an advancing Asiatic (Hittite) army of more than forty thousand to a standstill at the Syrian city of Kadesh. Any Asiatics crossing the border of Egypt proper in 1250 BC did so either as invitees or prisoners of war. The surviving *Ipuwer Papyrus* must have been a copy of an earlier document.

Copying documents in the ancient world had to be done by hand, a tedious and time consuming process. It could reasonably be justified only when important writing needed to be distributed or was in danger of loss due to deterioration. The *Ipuwer Papyrus* was centuries old when the surviving copy was made. Outdated propaganda or prophecy would not have merited the effort involved in making a copy that long after origination. The *Ipuwer Papyrus* must have had historical standing at the time the surviving copy was made. It must have reported events that were still seen as significant hundreds of years after their occurrence.

The surviving portion of the document, and large pieces including the ending are missing, does not provide a cohesive narrative. It is not specific as to the reason for the large influx of Asiatics. One fragment says that a foreign tribe from abroad has come to Egypt. Another laments that the tribes of the desert have become Egyptians everywhere and there are no Egyptians anywhere. Some number of the arriving Asiatics have overrun the marshlands, which were previously uninhabited. It is tempting to connect this with the Biblical occupation of the land of Goshen. That is speculation and is not supported by any evidence.

Some modern writers have been tempted to cite the *Ipuwer Papyrus* as support for the Biblical story of the exodus. This conclusion is not sustainable. The document clearly states that the Asiatics were coming into Egypt, not leaving. On a related note, it has been suggested that weather and seismic events following the Santorini eruption may explain the Biblical ten plagues of Egypt. This is another tempting avenue of speculation, but one that is best ignored for two reasons. First, the absence of supporting evidence has left Biblical scholars skeptical of the exodus story as presented in the Old Testament. Second, we have a direct written report of the impact of the Santorini eruption on Egypt. Speculation is not necessary.

Even in areas where Biblical lore has some credence we need to broaden our perspective to take account of historical reality. Understandably *Genesis* presents its central characters as heroic figures struggling to do the right thing in difficult circumstances. Not all of the residents of Canaan were high minded patriarchs seeking the best for their families. There were also tribes of predatory nomads, called Shasu. If famine dried up the rich pickings on the caravan routes of Canaan, Egypt would be a logical target of opportunity. The *Ipuwer Papyrus* reports roads becoming unsafe to travel, and murder becoming rampant.

The *Ipuwer Papyrus* is of particular value to our examination of the impact of the Santorini eruption because it does not limit itself to the problem of Asiatic influx. It presents the influx in the context of a larger calamity. Plague, we are told, is everywhere. The entire economic order has been upset. Formerly wealthy people have become poor in notable numbers.

Throughout history wealth has been based on the control of the capital assets used to produce income. In order for economic collapse to occur in the absence of war, pestilence or evaporation of resources, some wholesale destruction of the capital assets that supported the prosperity of the rich must have occurred. The *Ipuwer Papyrus* states specifically that critical commerce has been disrupted. The document laments that men no longer sail northward. Cedars and embalming oils are mentioned as lacking. Trading destinations are places as far away as Keftiu (previously defined as Crete, or more generally the Minoan Islands) are cited.

The lack of imported raw materials may be the source of the statement that no craftsmen work. The failure of maritime trade raises the possibility that Mediterranean seaports were among the assets damaged or destroyed. The violent tidal aftermath of the Santorini eruption would certainly have reached the Egyptian coast with sufficient force to wreak havoc. The failure of commerce may also explain the document's lamentation that rich fields went unplowed. Much of Egypt's agricultural output was grown for export. There would be no point growing crops that could not be transported for sale abroad.

Civil disorder is also addressed. According to the document, the poor of every town say let us suppress the rich among us. There are suggestions of looting. Ominous generalities tell the reader that the River (Nile) is blood and death is not lacking. Some of the document's statements are obscure. Reference is made to fire that has mounted up on high and goes against the enemies of the land. This could possibly refer to unusual weather triggered by the Santorini eruption, but it is not possible to draw any firm conclusions.

Overall the poor condition of the document and the difficulties of interpreting the references made by the author reduce the *Ipuwer Papyrus* to an intriguing set of hints at a possible impact of the Santorini eruption. It is not by itself a definitive proof. A good portion of the surviving elements are devoted to a plea to the king to restore *maat*, the Egyptian concept of peace and order, to the land. That is the source of a theory that the document is propaganda to support the actions of a heavy-handed Pharaoh. The idea fails on two counts. No specific Pharaoh is glorified, and reports of turmoil would have fallen on deaf ears if no actual turmoil existed. A second theory that the *Ipuwer Papyrus* is a prophecy foretelling the arrival of a good king to rescue the nation from turmoil also fails in the absence of actual turmoil.

The *Ipuwer Papyrus* clearly refers to a state of affairs prevalent at the time it was written. It contains no date to tell us when it was composed. The content does offer hints of when the events occurred. References to the kings of Upper and Lower Egypt suggest a date during the Hyksos period; since this was the time the country was divided along those lines. To align the timing with the Santorini eruption, we need to turn our attention to a larger and more official piece of writing.

EGYPT II:
THE TEMPEST STELA

In order to position the Santorini eruption in Egyptian chronology, we need a datable Egyptian reference to specific events related to the eruption. It is unlikely that we will find reference to the actual eruption. It would have been audible in Egypt, but the island of Santorini was too far away to be seen. Any reference would be to the destructive aftermath of the eruption, and possibly to related seismic activity in the Eastern Mediterranean fault zone.

This brings us to an examination of an artifact known as the *Tempest Stela*. Stela is a name given to an upright sculptured slab, often quite large, that is incised to memorialize a significant person, decree or event. Stelae provide a written record of the things considered most important by the ancient cultures that inscribed and erected them. They can answer questions of who, what, where and how. They can often be dated, either by the context in which they are found or by references in their content.

An example is the *Vulture Stela*. It was erected in Mesopotamia in the Third Millennium BC to commemorate the victory of the king of one city-state over another. The *Vulture Stela* is in the form of a large wall. The pictorial representations on its face show a uniformly equipped army drawn up in formation. This is the earliest evidence we have of the existence of a professional military establishment.

Archaeologists found the *Tempest Stela* in pieces at the third Pylon of the temple of Karnak at the old Egyptian capitol of Thebes between 1947 AD and 1951 AD. Placement in the premier temple in the nation's capitol was eloquent testimony to its importance. The *Stela* was reconstructed to the extent possible, although many pieces remain missing. Its surviving inscriptions were translated and finally published a decade and a half after its discovery.

The *Tempest Stela* and its content are worth our consideration for several reasons. The first is its sheer size and prominent placement. Taken together with the surviving inscriptions these suggest that the intent of the monument was to memorialize a singular catastrophic event in Egyptian history. The second is that the monument appears to be an eyewitness account of damage suffered as the result of the event, allowing us to evaluate its nature and severity. Lastly, and perhaps most important, is that it is known to have been inscribed and erected during the reign of Pharaoh Ahmose I. This fact positions us to approximate a date, based on Egyptian royal chronology, for the catastrophic event.

As often is the case in archeology, good fortune has been tempered by the ravages of time. The description of the storm and the overall impact of the event is the most damaged part of the *Stela*. The remaining fragments do provide insight into what happened. A few examples:

…the Gods caused the sky to come with a tempest. It caused darkness in the Western region…

The western region of the Nile Delta is the closest portion of Egypt to the Aegean Sea and the island of Santorini. Precise distribution of the ash cloud from the eruption is not known. If it reached Egypt the Western Nile Delta is the most likely area to suffer an obstruction of sunlight.

…houses and shelters…floating on the waters…for days.

This closely matches Twenty First Century AD television footage of the aftermath of the tsunami that struck the coast of Japan and initiated the Fukushima-Daichi nuclear disaster.

…with no one able to light the torch anywhere…These…surpass the power of the great god…

In Egypt gods were seen as omnipotent within their sphere of influence. Surpassing the power of the great god was probably the ultimate superlative available to the scribes of the time.

...the funerary concessions had been invaded (flooded?)...the sepulchral chambers had been damaged...the structures of the funerary enclosures had been undermined...the pyramids had collapsed...

These were structures designed to withstand any calamity known to the architects and engineers of the time. Intended as the eternal resting places of future inhabitants, they were built to the highest standards of quality.

...all that existed has been annihilated.

The *Stela* appears to refer at minimum to a widespread cataclysm of proportions not seen in living memory nor recounted in legend, possibly accompanied by one or more earthquakes. The *Stela* goes on to remark at length on the large sums the Pharaoh spent repairing the infrastructure damage and providing social welfare. An event of this scope and scale clearly had an abnormal cause. The geography and general description of the event are certainly right for it to be a direct result of the Santorini eruption. We need to look at whether the timing was right.

Although some dates in ancient Egypt can be pinned down fairly precisely, sometimes even to the day, others are moving targets. This results partly from the Egyptian practice of beginning a new set of dates when a new Pharaoh ascended to power. An example is the previously cited *Rhind Mathematical Papyrus*, which will figure prominently in the next chapter. The document is dated on its face to the fourth month of the thirty third regnal year of a ruler named Apophis. It is a compendium of Egyptian mathematical knowledge as it existed at the time of Apophis' reign.

Rather than being a traditional Pharaoh, Apophis was a Hyksos king who ruled at the same time as Theban Pharaohs. This allows us to place the document in the historical context of Hyksos control of the Nile Delta. Within this context we know only the general time frame of Apophis' rule. We do not know when he ascended to power, so we are not able to ascribe anything but a possible range of modern dates to the document.

In the case of the *Tempest Stela* we can derive an approximate modern date for the event memorialized based on the dates of the rule of the Theban Pharaoh Ahmose I, who commissioned the *Stela*. We are limited to approximation because the exact dates of rule are the subject of varying opinions among scholars. Each opinion is supported by some evidence, but none is persuasive.

Ahmose I has been closely studied. He is one of the most significant figures in ancient Egypt. The historian Manetho credited him as the founder of a new (Eighteenth) dynasty. In modern historical terms, that makes him the founding Pharaoh of what is now called the Egyptian New Kingdom, a period of about five hundred years, which represented the height of ancient Egypt's power. To understand the difficulty in pinning down the dates of Ahmose I's reign and the surrounding controversies, we will need to examine the efforts that have been made.

One effort involved anchoring the dates of Ahmose I's reign to an astronomical phenomenon called the Sothic Cycle or Canicular Period, an elapsed time of 1,461 Egyptian civil (as opposed to regnal) years, each consisting of 365 days, or 1,460 Julian years, each consisting of 365.25 days. This was close enough to the length of a modern year to be used with only minor adjustment. The method is based on ancient Egyptian records of observation of the star Sirius, part of the constellation Canis Major.

The rising of Sirius was important to the ancient Egyptians because it was thought to herald the annual flooding of the Nile. The apparent movement of Sirius in the heavens is noteworthy. It is the lowest (relative to the Earth's horizon) of the three bright stars that form the Winter Triangle. Stars higher in the heavens near the ecliptic (the arc the visible planets take across the night sky) move relative to an earthbound observer in a cycle that lasts just shorter than 72 years. Sirius' low position in the sky (about 40 degrees below the ecliptic) means that it will appear to rise in exactly the same place on the horizon over a much longer cycle. A new Sothic cycle is known to have begun in 139 AD. Reports of observations in ancient records theoretically allow the calculation of the date of that observation based on the difference in position from the known position of rising in 139 AD.

An observation of this rising is mentioned in writing associated with the reign of the Pharaoh Amenhotep I, the successor of Ahmose I. This observation is said to date Amenhotep I's reign to the period 1525 BC to 1504 BC. According to Manetho, Ahmose I ruled for twenty five years, four months. One surviving piece of contemporary documentation is dated on its face as being from the twenty second year of the reign of Ahmose I, lending credence to Manetho's time line. This observation would place the twenty five year reign of Ahmose I at 1550 to 1525 BC.

Unfortunately there are several problems associated with both the dating method and its application in this case. The first is that the date established by observation of the rising of Sirius is highly sensitive to the latitude at which the observation is taken. We do not know the location of the observation in question. The current dating assumes that the observation was made at the traditional capitol of Thebes. If it were actually made at a city in the Nile Delta, Heliopolis for example, the resulting dates for the reign of Amenhotep I would be twenty years earlier. Other locations could produce greater variations.

The methodology also assumes that the ancient Egyptian civil calendar remained unchanged over thousands of years. A single calendar revision would invalidate the entire calculation. Without specific knowledge of the nature and timing of revision(s) it would be impossible to correct the dating, and unwise to accept it without corroboration or assurance of the absence of revision.

Most damaging is the fact that the record of observation associated with Amenhotep I makes no mention of any specific Pharaoh. It was assigned to his reign by modern scholars based on the best related information available. The information that has come down to us from the early years of the Egyptian New Kingdom is random and fragmentary, and can be subject to multiple interpretations. There is no certainty that the best guess is the right guess.

Given complete information, the Sothic cycle is a valid dating tool. We are not fortunate enough to have that in the case of the reign of Ahmose I. At present we have no other astronomical observations from the period that would lend themselves to calculation of a corresponding modern date. We will have to accept that, given currently available information, there is no way to derive at a modern date for the reign of Ahmose I that is anchored in a verifiable astronomical phenomenon.

Absent a precisely derived and astronomically anchored date, the next best alternative would be a narrow date range established by radiocarbon dating of one or more artifacts known to be from the reign of Ahmose I. This brings us to item number 61057 in the Cairo Museum catalog. The item is the mummy of a robustly built male. The head has become detached but is still present. A height of five feet six inches would place him at the upper end of the normal range of Egyptian men of the New Kingdom. Medical inspection placed his age at death around 35 years.

The mummy was not recovered from an original royal burial. It was discovered in 1881 AD among a cache of royal mummies that included the warrior Pharaoh Thutmoses III, who expanded the Egyptian empire to its greatest extent, and Ramses II, the longest ruling and best known Pharaoh of the New Kingdom. The name Ahmose I was found in hieratic Egyptian on the mummy wrappings of item 61057. Radiocarbon analysis was performed. Based on the results a range from 1570 BC to 1544 BC was established for the start of the approximate twenty five year reign of Ahmose I.

The radiocarbon analysis has never been questioned, but a cautionary note is in order regarding the presentation of the results. The gold standard for such results is a 95 percent confidence level. This means that the results are expected to be wrong only 5 percent of the time. For comparison, consider the probability of a fair coin toss coming up heads four successive times, not a particularly rare occurrence. The odds are one divided by two (the probability of a single occurrence) raised to the fourth (number of occurrences) power. This is equal to 6.25 percent, very close to the gold standard confidence level. This standard, dating from the 1920's AD, has recently come under hostile scrutiny by the scientific establishment. This is one reason why archaeologists seek corroboration from other dating approaches.

While radiocarbon results for 61057 have an excellent chance of being correct, several issues exist with the subject mummy. The wrappings containing the name of Ahmose I also contain the name of a later Pharaoh, Piendjem II. This means that the mummy was rewrapped after original mummification. We are dependent on the people who did the rewrapping for correct identification of the mummy. We do not know what information was available to them or by what process the identification was arrived at.

The coffin in which the mummy was found was not of the type used in royal burials. It was, however, dated to the Eighteenth Dynasty. This makes it unlikely that the original was a royal coffin that was ruined by grave robbers stripping gold inlay and replaced later when the mummy was re-wrapped. The coffin in which item 61057 was found was probably an artifact of the original burial.

Another issue is the posing of the mummy. Royal funerals were highly stylized and the mummies carefully prepared according to a set formula. Pharaohs were buried in the pose we are familiar with from the exhibition of the funeral artifacts of Tutankamun. The arms were crossed over the torso and the hands held a rod and a flail, symbols of royal power in Egypt. The mummy identified as Ahmose I was not posed in this fashion, making it all but certain this was not a royal mummy. As a side note on the topic, the absence of royal pose was not the result of a hasty burial. Tutankamun, whose mummy was correctly posed, was prepared and buried in haste, as evidenced by fire damage to the mummy and placement in a chamber that appears to have been intended for a lesser royal.

Casting further doubt on the identification of item 61057 was an X-ray analysis conducted of royal mummies in the late 1980's AD. The craniofacial morphology of the mummy cataloged 61057 differed significantly from that of Sequenenre Tao II, the father (or perhaps grandfather) of Ahmose I, and from that of Ahmose I's sister. Although the mummy currently resides in the Luxor Museum labeled as Ahmose I, a significant body of evidence suggests that we have the correct radiocarbon dates for the wrong person.

In the absence of an astronomically anchored date or uncontested radiocarbon dating for the reign of Ahmose I, we are left with contemporary records. The reference most commonly used to date the reign of Pharaohs prior to Ramses II, who came to power in 1279 BC, is a document called the *Turin King List*. The document is believed to have been compiled during the reign of Ramses II. It is the most comprehensive New Kingdom list of Egyptian rulers and the length of their reigns currently available. The durations of reign are primarily given in round years, although some are carried out to month and day. The list was not official. It was written on the back of an outdated papyrus tax roll, suggesting it was intended for informal use in some minor administrative or ceremonial role. This may be an advantage. Lack of formality may have shielded the list from the contemporary bias often found in official documents.

The papyrus arrived at the Turin Museum in 1824 AD in appalling condition. The medium had disintegrated into some 160 fragments. Subsequent reconstruction efforts have established that both the beginning and end of the document are missing. Studies of the reconstructed portion, and there are many gaps, show that a good number of the names on the list correspond to names on monuments or other documents. This level of vetting is enough to provide confidence in the list as a source of general chronology.

Unfortunately there are discrepancies. Not all of the names correspond. That calls into question the precision of the document when addressing specific chronological events, in our case the dates of the reign of Ahmose I. Additional fragments of the papyrus have been found. A revised list is expected to be produced when these can be appropriately fitted and the fitting vetted. That may or may not produce a verifiable date for the reign of Ahmose I.

The only other surviving king list covering the period we are looking at is the *Abydos Table,* found on a wall of the tomb of Pharaoh Seti I. This is a set of 76 cartouches, oval enclosures surrounding the hieroglyphic names of Pharaohs. The length of their reigns is not provided, so it is impossible to count backward from a known date. In addition, several well known Pharaohs were omitted, including Hatshepsut, Akhenaten and Tutankamun. This may have to do with uneasiness over legitimacy of succession. Tutankamun died without issue. The throne was taken over by the Vizier, Ai. Following Ai was a general named Horemheb, who founded the Rameseid Dynasty during which the *Abydos Table* was compiled. As with any contemporary writing, we are in danger of being told only what the contemporary writer or his patron wanted known.

With the elimination of contemporary writing, we have exhausted the reliable sources that might be used to establish precise dates for the reign of Ahmose I. We do have Manetho's construction of Egyptian dynasties. This, and supporting contemporary writing, allows us to place Ahmose I in the correct order of rule and provides a credible statement of his length of reign. It does not offer modern dates for the beginning and end of his rule. And it does not cite the source documents on which Manetho's construction was based.

We have a date no later than 1600 BC established by radiocarbon dating and corroborated by dendrochronology for the Santorini eruption. Currently we have a choice of reign dates for Ahmose I. 1539 to 1514 BC is disputed as often as it is accepted. 1550 to 1525 BC was derived by a questionable application of the Sothic cycle. Radiocarbon results suggest a date of ascension as early as 1570 BC. Regrettably the remains tested are probably not those of Ahmose I. None of the suggested dates are demonstrably valid. None of the supporting arguments are sufficiently persuasive to place the beginning of Ahmose I's reign after the 1600 BC Santorini eruption.

That brings us back to the subject of the *Tempest Stela*. The *Stela* was inscribed and mounted to memorialize important events and achievements during the reign of Ahmose I. The power of the Santorini eruption and its proximity to Egypt make it likely that the aftermath was a defining factor in the rule of whoever was Pharaoh at the time. It would have been to the Pharaoh's advantage to detail to both the gods and the people of Egypt the forces of nature confronting him and his success in overcoming them. The *Tempest Stela* appears to be part of that narrative.

It seems likely that the *Ipuwer Papyrus* is a less formal and more comprehensive account of the misfortune that befell Egypt in the aftermath of the Santorini eruption. Ahmose I was the Pharaoh chosen by fate to cope with the calamity. Examination of the history of his reign will give us a detailed look at the outcome of the eruption for Egypt then and in the future.

EGYPT III: EXPULSION AND EMPIRE

Pharaohs, including Ahmose I, accumulated multiple names during their lifetimes. Often royal names went beyond simple identification to suggest metaphysical alliances or to memorialize activities. The common name Ahmose is a combination of the moon god *Ah* and the word *mose*, which is a general reference to offspring. The name is generally translated to *Born of the Moon God*. Upon his ascension to the throne of Egypt at the age of ten Ahmose I acquired the throne name Nebpehtire, which translates to *The Lord of Strength is Re*, and under which he is listed on the *Abydos Table* and other official writings. This name existed mainly as a formal title of address. Two other names give some insight into the notable events of Ahmose I's reign. The name Tjestway means *He Who Binds Together the Two Lands*, thought to be a reference to his expulsion of the Hyksos and the re-unification of Egypt under a Theban Pharaoh. Aakheperu means *Great of Developments* and likely refers to the infrastructure building and re-establishment of trade that occurred during his reign.

At the beginning of his reign, as a minor child, Ahmose I was a figurehead under the regency of his mother, Ahhotep. The regency inherited a land divided in more ways than one. The Hyksos ruled Northern Egypt, essentially the Nile Delta. A few military sallies and a declaration of victory by the predecessor Pharaoh Kamose had done nothing to dislodge the Hyksos. The royal counselors of Southern Egypt, the portion ruled by

Ahmose I from Thebes, were divided on whether to accept the de-facto partition of Egypt as the most practical compromise or attempt to force re-unification. In keeping with modern convention we will refer to Southern Egypt, the portion closest to the head waters of the Nile, as Upper Egypt and the Nile Delta as Lower Egypt.

Ahhotep appears to have focused the efforts of her regency on consolidating the power of the Theban throne. No detailed narrative of her activities survives, so we must rely on the outcome to draw conclusions. During her regency the Hyksos remained in Lower Egypt. It is not clear whether this was the result of active containment by the Theban throne. It may be that the Hyksos had no designs on Upper Egypt, or that they postponed expansion to address other priorities. Ahhotep's regency did provide the wherewithal for Ahmose I to strike against the Hyksos when the opportunity presented itself.

It appears that the opportunity came in the form of a singular event. Actions by the prior Pharaoh, Kamose, establish that the Theban monarchy had the means to conduct offensive military operations against the Hyksos. The failure of Kamose's operations and the absence of a Hyksos counter-offensive suggest the existence of a balance of power. Some event had to shift that balance in the Theban's favor to make a new attempt at expulsion practical.

Ahmose I's age when he began the long process of expulsion is not known. Since he died around age 35, the Hyksos expulsion would have consumed a sizeable portion of his adult life. Even if he had reached maturity when it began, he would have been young and would have had to rely heavily on his senior military commanders for advice and execution. An established habit of delegation and reliance would have served him well in meeting the daunting building challenges he confronted later in his reign.

Very little is known about the initial phase of Ahmose I's campaign against the Hyksos. Most of our knowledge comes from a cursory military narrative written on the back of the previously mentioned Hyksos document, the *Rhind Mathematical Papyrus*. The original document was prepared in the 4th month of the 33rd regnal year of the Hyksos king Apophis. It is usually and reasonably assumed that the mathematical knowledge it contained was not exclusive to Upper or Lower Egypt.

Rather that the document was a technical summary of public knowledge accumulated over centuries. As such, the verso was simply a convenient place to write the military narrative.

The military narrative written on the back of the *Rhind Mathematical Papyrus* is dated simply to the 11th regnal year. Since this cannot be a reference to Apophis, it is assumed to be that of Khamudi, who succeeded Apophis as ruler of the Hyksos. We cannot firmly fix the dates of rule of either Hyksos king, so we cannot derive a modern date for the military narrative on the basis of the dates presented on the face or the verso of the document.

Since the narrative is Hyksos in origin, it cannot offer strategic insight into Theban activities. On a more positive note, its Hyksos origin insulates it from the propaganda often encountered in Theban writing. Ahmose I is not mentioned by name in the narrative, but is cited simply as the Prince of the South. The reference is generally taken to be Ahmose I, based on other information. He was the Theban Pharaoh of record at the time associated with the Hyksos Expulsion. One of his names refers to him as unifier of Egypt. Manetho credits him with expelling the Hyksos from Egypt.

The military narrative reads like a set of brief after-action diary entries, one of which is translated to read:

Regnal year 11, second month of shomu, Heliopolis was entered

The second month of Shomu corresponds most closely with modern July. Egyptian campaigns normally began in early April, just after the completion of harvest. A later start may indicate that the opportunity to move against the Hyksos came about unexpectedly.

Heliopolis is a later Greek name meaning City of the Sun, and is used by modern convention. It was a Delta city located just outside of modern Cairo. It was a significant landmark in ancient Egyptian culture, thought to be the place where the gods first entered Earth.

For Ahmose I it had a more practical value. Anyone invading the Nile Delta from the south faced a logistical problem. The only route by which large numbers of troops and their supporting supplies could be moved expeditiously was the Nile River. This convenient avenue of travel would become a bottleneck when any sizable movement was involved. For Ahmose I's assault against Lower Egypt, Heliopolis was a logical staging area. He could move troops and supplies down the Nile piecemeal, as the limits of transport and facilities permitted, and then marshal his forces and stockpile his logistical requirements at Heliopolis for coming operations.

The narrative continues:

First month of Akhet, day 23, the Southern Prince broke into Tjaru or, in alternative translation, *First month of Akhet, 23rd day, He of the South strikes against Sile*

The first month of Akhet, day 23, corresponds most closely with a date in modern October. Tjaru and Sile are place (garrison) names. In geographical context, the narrative entry essentially means that Ahmose I's opening maneuver after consolidating his forces at Heliopolis was to seize the fortifications that controlled of the Horus Road at Egypt's eastern border. The Horus Road was the main thoroughfare from Canaan into Egypt. Seizure of the border fortifications allowed Ahmose I to close the road to overland traffic from Canaan.

Although the narrative does not say so, it has been widely concluded that the closure of the Horus Road was intended to block any flow of supplies or reinforcements from Canaan to the Hyksos capitol of Avaris and other strongholds in the Nile Delta prior to Ahmose I's assault. That fits neatly with the modern military philosophy called coring out, which dictates pre-emptive strikes against potential reinforcement prior to an assault. In the context of Ahmose I's operations against the Hyksos, it can be valid only under very specific conditions.

The main issue is that Ahmose I had only a riverine navy. He did not possess the seagoing fleet necessary to mount a naval blockade against the ports on the Mediterranean coast. Those ports were under Hyksos control. Under normal circumstances there was extensive maritime trade throughout the Eastern Mediterranean. Avaris and other targeted Hyksos cities could have been supplied and/or reinforced by sea if necessary. Ahmose I's blockade of the Horus Road could have been effective in isolating the Nile Delta only if all of the ports had already been damaged to the point where they were unusable, or destroyed completely.

The only known force capable of such simultaneous destruction along the entire Egyptian coast during the Middle Bronze Age was the tidal aftermath of the Santorini eruption. The tsunami, travelling at five hundred miles an hour, would have reached the Egyptian coast with its fury intact. Every port and every cove suitable as a harbor would have been sucked dry, its waters added to the inbound wave. The force of the inrushing water would have ripped every scrap of infrastructure loose from its foundations and swept it inland to be deposited helter skelter as the waters receded.

It was the destructive aftermath of the Santorini eruption that gave the Theban forces of Ahmose I the opportunity to expel the Hyksos from Egypt after his predecessors had suffered the indignity of failure.

The conclusion that blockading the Horus Road was one element of a strategy to defeat the Hyksos is not in keeping with the times. The normal Bronze Age approach to reducing a fortified urban area was to block off the immediate vicinity. The goal was to either starve the defenders into submission or to weaken them to the point they could be overcome by main assault or superior tactics. The defenders would call on any available ally in the region to help lift the siege. As portrayed in Homer's *Iliad,* the result was a protracted process involving repeated heavy fighting in the area of the objective. In the case of Ahmose I's assault on Avaris, the Pharaoh could ill-afford commit a sizeable portion of his force to a distant blockade.

It seems likely that a general blockade of the Horus Road had a purpose beyond simply being part of a strategy to expel the Hyksos. To make a best guess at the purpose we can combine the effect of the blockade with what we know from contemporary writing. Seizing the border fortifications would cut off all flow of migrants from Canaan, regardless of whether the migrants were reinforcements or refugees. That sounds very much like a royal response to the lament of the *Ipuwer Papyrus* to the effect that Egypt was being overrun by Asiatics, and to the writer's plea to the Pharaoh to address the threat.

That conclusion supports the indications raised by stories in *Genesis* that volcanic winter produced by the Santorini eruption sent starving Canaanites into Egypt in overwhelming numbers. It also places the activity in the historical context of the Hyksos expulsion. Not only did the Santorini eruption create opportunity for the Theban ruler. It also brought problems that he had to address. Ahmose I reacted both to stem the flow would-be migrants at the border and to take advantage of the damage done to the infrastructure of Lower Egypt to move against the Hyksos.

Ahmose I's assault on the Hyksos capitol of Avaris is memorialized to a degree in the funeral inscriptions of one of his officers, another Ahmose, son of Ebana. The Pharaoh Ahmose I mounted three unsuccessful attacks against Avaris. At that point circumstances intervened. He was forced to postpone his efforts against the Hyksos in order to quell a rebellion in another part of Egypt. Ahmose I's fourth attack against Avaris succeeded. Additional campaigning was required before Ahmose I was able to complete the defeat of the Hyksos by reducing their last stronghold at Sharuhen, in Gaza, after a three year siege. That portion of the narrative of the Hyksos expulsion does conform to Bronze Age practice.

Ahmose I did not stop with the expulsion of the Hyksos from Egypt. He pressed his campaign north into Canaan and Syria. His northernmost known penetration was to a town thought to be near Byblos, a city on the East Coast of the Mediterranean at about the same latitude as the island of Cyprus. This is documented on an ostracon from the tomb of his wife. Ostracon is a term used by archaeologists to describe a fragment of pottery with symbols on it.

Ahmose I did not use his military advantage to exploit Canaan, as Pharaohs traditionally did in the gold bearing land of Nubia to the south. Rather he laid waste to the cities he conquered. This policy makes little sense, unless the land was already devastated by natural disaster to the point where the cost of holding it exceeded the value to be gained from exploiting it. Conquest and spoiling sent a clear message to any Canaanites tempted to view Egypt as a land of opportunity, as well as degrading any capability to make mischief.

As for the Hyksos, Ahmose I obliterated all trace of their rule in Lower Egypt. It is probable that only the Hyksos elite were actually expelled. The general population was a source of manual labor, exploitable skill sets and commercial contacts. Those would be essential for the immediate term in repairing the damage to the unified nation, and for ensuring its prosperity in the longer term. It was to Ahmose I's advantage to integrate the Hyksos majority into the Egyptian population. Destroying links to the Hyksos past was a step in that direction.

The Hyksos expulsion is thought to have been completed no later than the nineteenth year of the twenty five year reign of Ahmose I. He then turned his attention to construction projects and to the expansion of trade. The massive scale of his construction efforts is indicated by contemporary writing. The need for materials was great enough to require him to re-open quarries and mines. The scope of trade can be illustrated by a few examples. Oxen were brought in from Canaan for heavy construction work. Cedar was imported from Byblos and lapis lazuli from as far away as Central Asia. Minoan art work has been found in a palace constructed in the captured city of Avaris.

It is unlikely that Ahmose I simply woke up one morning and decided to build things and expand trade. An expensive series of construction projects, particularly in the aftermath of an expensive military campaign, would have been driven only by pressing need. The most likely source of such a need in that time period was widespread infrastructure devastation caused by the Santorini eruption and damage resulting from the lengthy campaign against the Hyksos. The need to expand trade is also unusual. The norm is for economies to overheat and expand during wartime and cool down and contract following hostilities. The end of the Hyksos expulsion should have brought about a reduction in commerce. Ahmose I must have faced an unusual set of circumstances. Conceivably those described in the *Ipuwer Papyrus.*

In summary, the actions and achievements of Ahmose I are best explained when viewed in the context of the Santorini eruption. They are difficult to explain otherwise. There was no reason for him to block the Horus road at the Egyptian border unless he was facing an overwhelming influx of refugees from Canaan. There was no reason for such an influx unless some disaster had befallen Canaan. There was no reason, given the long prevailing balance of power, for him to be able to defeat and expel the Hyksos when they had defied his predecessors for decades. Something must have changed in the interim to weaken the Hyksos. As rulers of the portion of Egypt adjacent to the Mediterranean coast, their infrastructure was most vulnerable to the tidal aftermath of the eruption.

The search for physical evidence supporting the impact of the Santorini eruption on Egypt has been frustrating. The country escaped volcanic winter by virtue of being out of the wind patterns that carried the stratospheric sulfate aerosol veil. Any evidence of tidal damage has been destroyed by repairs which themselves have been buried by the natural deposits of thirty six centuries. Egypt is in an earthquake prone area, so that no seismic damage could be specifically linked to the Santorini eruption. The particulate ejecta from the volcano were heavier than air and most had settled out before reaching Egypt. Small amounts of pumice found during the excavation of Avaris were chemically traced to the Santorini eruption. The pumice was dated at 1540 BC; however this was based on disputed dating of the relevant stratum at Avaris.

Rather than dating the Santorini eruption according to the currently accepted range for the reign of Ahmose I, we would be on firmer ground anchoring the reign of Ahmose I in the time of the Santorini eruption, around 1600 BC, and adjusting relevant portions of the current Egyptian chronology to fit. Upsetting the decades of research that have gone into establishing the current chronology may sound like academic heresy, but it is not without precedent. In the 1970's AD the chronology had to be adjusted by a quarter century. As it turned out, this movement brought the Egyptian chronology into better alignment with dates being established in other areas of the Eastern Mediterranean world. The same is quite probably true of anchoring the beginning of New Kingdom Egypt in the aftermath of the Santorini eruption.

Without the Santorini eruption it is unlikely that Egyptian New Kingdom would have arisen. The expulsion of the Hyksos in the wake of the eruption had ramifications that went beyond the borders of Egypt. Long term engagement with an entrenched Hyksos dynasty required the Pharaoh to raise and maintain a large standing army capable of expeditionary deployment beyond the traditional operational area of the Nile River. This military organization remained after the victory over the Hyksos. Ahmose I used it to lay waste to parts of Canaan. Later Pharaohs would put it to more ambitious use in the establishment of an empire.

Expansion began in earnest during the co-regency of Hatshepsut and Thutmosis III in the Mid-Fifteenth Century BC. Hatshepsut, the apparent senior of the two and one of Egypt's few woman rulers, focused on expanding trade, in particular to the south, via the Red Sea. With her passing, Thutmosis III assumed sole power. He was more interested in conquest than commerce. Technology favored his aspirations. The composite, compound curve bow of the time could place arrows effectively at three hundred yards. The chariot had evolved from the clumsy cart pictured on the wall of the tomb of Ahmose, son of Ebana, to the light, maneuverable, six spoke archery platform that ruled the Middle Eastern battlefields of the Late Bronze Age. Armies so equipped possessed an overwhelming advantage.

Over the span of more than a decade Thutmosis III drove the Egyptian army north through Canaan and continued his advance into Syria. This time the objective was occupation. The Santorini eruption fundamentally altered the course of Egyptian history, bringing centuries of imperial power and commercial prosperity. In turn, Egyptian imperial power altered the course of history in neighboring lands.

Children of conquered rulers were taken to Egypt, raised within Egyptian culture and returned to rule as Egyptian vassals. Local military levies were raised under Egyptian command. Merchants were integrated into the Egyptian trade network. Harsh punishment was meted out for piracy and for the plunder of caravans. The result was an Egyptian empire that controlled the gold fields of Nubia in the south, the agricultural wealth of the Nile and several hundred miles of Mediterranean coastline.

In spite of a stabilizing Egyptian influence the situation in the Eastern Mediterranean following the Santorini eruption grew fluid and perilous. The Aegean catastrophe set in motion the growth of other great powers. Eventually Pharaoh Ramses II would be locked in perhaps the greatest battle of the Late Bronze Age to preserve the Egyptian empire. A century later Ramses III would be forced to defend the borders of Egypt itself against a determined and ruthless invasion force. Even in defeat, the enemies of Egypt would have a say in the future of civilization.

THE LOST EMPIRE

Today the Hittites enjoy a secure place in history, even to the point of having television documentaries made about them. Such was not always the case. The name Hittite comes from obscure references in Judeo-Christian scripture. One has a patriarch buying a burial plot from a Hittite. Another cites the Hittites as enemies of the Egyptians. Nothing more is said. Generations of biblical scholars were divided over whether the Hittites were a minor Syrian tribe or merely a figment of some priestly writer's imagination.

Other scholars poring over ancient Egyptian diplomatic correspondence found mention of a people called *Kheti*, but had no idea who they were. The state of knowledge changed in the early years of the Twentieth Century AD. Archaeologists explored a ruined city above a forbidding Halys River gorge in the Taurus Mountains of Turkey. The city was the ancient Hittite capitol, Hattusas. It contained an archive of thousands of inscribed tablets that would shed light on an empire that once ruled much of the Eastern Mediterranean.

The current fashion is to classify the Hittites as the warlike descendants of a migration of people called Yamnaya from the Steppes of Russia that began about 3000 BC. This group had domesticated horses and made use of the wheel, which gave them superior mobility. They swept westward into Europe, overwhelming and displacing the existing residents and imposing their Indo-European language. There is a core of truth in this scenario. The Steppe migration has been validated by both DNA and archaeological findings. As we will see in a later chapter, migration from Eurasia did have a prominent role to play in the aftermath of the Santorini eruption. There is no evidence that it had a role in the ancestry of the Hittites. We need to be careful how much we infer from the limited information available.

A later example of piling too many conclusions on too little information is the British legend of King Arthur. When the Romans abandoned Britain around 410 AD written history disappeared. The following two centuries were known as the Dark Ages. The long prevailing theory was that hordes of Angles and Saxons flooded in from Europe to fill the power vacuum left by the Romans, overwhelming the existing population by violence and attempting to take over the entire country. According to the writings of Geoffrey of Monmouth some centuries later, a king named Arthur arose to lead the British opposition and stopped the westward expansion of the invaders in a series of battles. This story, stripped of its sex and violence, seemed to fit with a general north-south dividing line known to exist in the British population. It became accepted as a core of truth gilded with dramatic embellishment.

Recent scientific analysis has called the entire scenario into question. DNA of the British population has been exhaustively studied. Even in the supposedly conquered areas, Anglo-Saxon DNA has contributed only about ten percent. Of the disinterred human remains from the period, a sample that numbers over one thousand, only a minimal percentage show signs of trauma. The numbers are in line with modern figures for crime and accident. No battlefields have been identified. Tintagel, in Cornwall, where the whole Arthur business is said to have begun, has been painstakingly excavated. Archaeological finds show the primary activities in the area were open pit tin mining and maritime commerce. If King Arthur existed, his function was probably closer to that of a modern corporate CEO than an Iron Age warlord.

Applying the lesson of the Arthur legend to theories of the origin of the Hittites, the need for caution becomes evident. We have no Hittite genome. This means there can be no direct DNA trace of the Hittites to the Steppe migration. DNA research into European horse breeds established that there was no central point of domestication. If the Yamnaya had been exclusive in introducing domesticated horses into Europe, there should be a traceable line of descent to modern horses. The concept of a migration from the sparsely populated Steppes conquering and replacing the far denser population of Europe fails on the basis of simple arithmetic.

DNA analysis of the Steppe people also established that they were carriers of pneumonic plague. The absence of immunity among European populations may have had more to do with the success of the Steppe migration in replacing the indigenous population than any warlike action on the part of the migrants. A modern corollary is the European introduction of the smallpox and other contagions that ravaged the native population of the Americas. Pissarro and Cortes are prominently pictured in histories of the conquest of the New World. The real conquistadores could be seen only through a powerful microscope.

If the Hittites were Yamnaya migrating into the Taurus Mountains, as the theory suggests, they would have brought plague with them. There would have been a large scale replacement of population as there was in Europe. There is no evidence of such a replacement. Nor is there any archaeological evidence of migration as the source of the Hittites.

Scholars have suggested that Hittite use of an Indo-European language is traceable to the Steppe migration. Indo-European is not an actual language. Rather it is a family of languages thought to have descended from a single ancient language that no longer exists. Since the source language pre-dated writing, no physical proof of its existence remains. Efforts have been made to trace backward from languages that either are in use today or have been written down in the past by using similarities in vocabulary. These efforts have not produced a consensus. It is not known how the Yamnaya came to use an Indo-European language.

A key argument used in tracing the spread of Indo-European into Europe by way of the Yamnaya migration is the fact that European languages have related words for the components of wheeled vehicles. A word for axle, for example, would be unnecessary unless wagons were in common use. It was the Yamnaya who brought wagons, and with them the associated vocabulary into Europe. Hittite Indo-European did not share the Yamnaya vocabulary for describing the components of wheeled vehicles. The Hittites did make extensive use of such vehicles.

The Hittites themselves said their language was Nesili, which it originated locally from the Anatolian city of Nesa. They also made use of Akkadian, which is classed as an Afro-Asian language, and another local Indo-European language called Luwian. At least one study supports the hypothesis that Indo-European originated in Anatolia. This study suggests a date for the source Indo-European language of 5500 BC, well before the rise of the Yamnaya.

The Hittite archives establish that their culture was multi-lingual (by necessity) and beholden to no one source for spoken or written communication. Nesili and Akkadian were written in cuneiform, which is typical of areas to the south of Anatolia. Luwian was written in hieroglyphics of uncertain origin.

A quick look at modern language shows that we would be on shaky ground drawing conclusions from form of transmission, storage or presentation. We normally think of English in terms of a twenty six character alphabet augmented by a decimal numbering system. This was reduced to two characters, a dot and a dash, when the invention of telegraphy enabled the electrical transmission of messages. This book was written in another electrically based two character representation of English, the on-or-off switch positions used in the binary code of computers. Other languages, both related and unrelated to English and the English alphabet, have been reduced to these two character representations.

Modern scribes (telegraphers) transfer messages into two character code using a key and transcribe it back into the original alpha-numeric character representation from a sounder or beat frequency oscillator. Computers automate this process with a keyboard and screen. The astronomical number or transistors (on-off switches) embedded in a single memory chip allow a sizeable library to fit into a pocket-sized electronic tablet. Messaging is often stored exclusively in binary format. Modern subpoenas and warrants include e-mail archives and computer storage devices. Written form is as likely to result from necessity or convenience as it is from heredity.

Much of what we know about the Hittites comes to us in their own handwriting. Most of the contemporary Hittite writing we currently possess was set down during the Hittite imperial period, stretching from about 1450 BC to 1250 BC, well after the Santorini eruption. Included in the Hittite archive, however, are copies of earlier writings. The copies were commissioned by a ruler during the Hittite New Kingdom. We can reasonably infer, based on their official status, that the copies are accurate. We can further infer that the documents copied were seen by knowledgeable Hittites as having recorded pivotal events in their history.

To trace the Hittites from their roots we will need to look at Assyrian records from a city called Kultepe. Writing generally lumped under the title the *Kultepe Texts,* consisting of about 20,000 cuneiform tablets recovered to date, traces activity in an adjacent trading center. The center had the general name Karun, an Akkadian word meaning port, which had been corrupted over time to refer to any area where commerce was the primary activity. Adjoining Karun was a lower city called Kanes or Kanesa. This city became Nesa in the writing of the Hittites. It was well established before their first recorded appearance.

The *Kultepe Texts* contain the first mention of Indo-European names in the area and, although written in old Assyrian, contain words borrowed from Indo-European. This is also the first known rendering of Indo-European in cuneiform. Kultepe appears to have been the administrative center for Assyrian commerce in Anatolia from the Twenty First to the Eighteenth Centuries BC. Commerce requires written records. This may have been the source of the Hittite written language, Indo-European rendered in cuneiform, which they called Nesili, or the language of Nesa. As in modern times, the form of writing appears to have been an outgrowth of both necessity and convenience.

Additional knowledge of the precursor history of the Hittites is drawn from later copies of much older Hittite texts made during the New Kingdom. One of these concerns a king called Pitkhana, ruler of a city called Kussara, the location of which remains undiscovered. Pitkhana conquered a large number of cities, including Nesa. His son, Annita, made his capitol at Nesa. He is also credited with burning the then existing city of Hattusas and placing a curse on it. These events are now thought to presage the rise of the Hittite kingdom. The best currently available evidence suggests that the two kings were part of a non-Indo-European speaking people called Hattians. When the Hittites came to power they would refer to themselves as Rulers of the Land of Hatti.

The beginning of Hittite history, at least as seen by the Hittites, is drawn from a document called the *Edict of Telepinus*. Telepinus was the last ruler of the Hittite Old Kingdom, which is generally taken to have ended around 1500 BC. As part of his legacy, he set down the early history of the Hittites. The earliest member of the Hittite royal line we know of is a king named Labarnas. It is not known whether he founded the Hittite dynasty, but it is clear from independent references that such a person did exist. He established his seat of government at the (presumably rebuilt) city of Hattusas, and took the name Hattusilis. He was known as King of Hattusas and Man of Kussara.

Under Hattusilis the Hittites waged several successful military campaigns and extended their influence into what is now Northern Syria. Hattusilis is said to have boasted that he made the sea his frontier, presumably a reference to stretching the Hittite kingdom as far as the Mediterranean. This would have been little more than a toehold. The principal power in Northern Syria remained the kingdom of Yamhad, based in the city of Aleppo.

Hattusilis harbored ambitions that exceeded his abilities. He organized an assault against the kingdom of Arzawa in the rich agricultural lands to the west, only to find himself under pressure from the Hurrians to the east. He was forced to abandon his westward expansion to retake his eastern territories. He continued to fight in Northern Syria, facing organized opposition from both the Hurrians and Aleppo. In the end he returned, seriously wounded, to his old capitol of Kussara. There he appointed his grandson, Mursulis I, to follows him as king. Mursulis I proved to be an able military commander. He won a decisive victory over the Hurrians and subsequently inflicted a similar defeat on Aleppo.

That brings us to an unusual event in Hittite history. Mursulis I did not pursue further victory in Northern Syria, or move to exploit the wealth of nearby Arzawa. Instead he mounted an unsuccessful assault on the distant city of Babylon, attempting a march through the Taurus Mountains. He followed this up during the next campaign season with a successful raid on the city, moving some five hundred miles along the

Euphrates River to accomplish his objective. The date is of particular interest to us. The city fell at approximately the same time as the death of Samsuditana, the last king of the first dynasty of Babylon. That allows the event to be reliably dated to 1595 BC according to the Babylonian long chronology, which we will examine in detail in a later chapter.

Mursulis I's assault on Babylon has gone unexplained by historians. There seemed to be no reason for him to abandon successful operations in the area of Northern Syria or to ignore the potential rich pickings in the Anatolian kingdom of Arzawa to undertake a risky and expensive foray against the powerful capitol of Sumeria half a thousand miles distant. And then to mount a second attempt when the first failed.

As king of the Hittites and direct human representative of the storm god, Mursulis I appeared omnipotent. In fact he was the slave of economic necessity. His military adventures had to pay the cost of maintaining his army and provide enough excess to support his nation. Abandoning lucrative action close to his homeland would make sense only if the rich plunder and tribute there had suddenly evaporated.

The agricultural and commercial economies of Anatolia and Syria had matured over many centuries. They had withstood storms, drought, pestilence and earthquakes. They had flourished in spite of war and adapted to political change. A long standing and wide spread economy does not simply cease to exist overnight for no reason. Some highly unusual event must have brought massive crop failure in Syria and across Anatolia, and an abrupt end to the rich trade in the Eastern Mediterranean.

Such occurrences are the logical outcome of the Santorini eruption. The ejecta could lock large areas to the east of the island in volcanic winter. Tidal action had the power to produce comprehensive destruction of commercial ports along the Eastern Mediterranean coast. In the absence of goods moved by seaborne trade, and with little in the way of exportable agricultural produce to move, overland commerce would have withered. Physical evidence, in the form of ash fall chemically associated with the Santorini eruption, has been found in Anatolia. A date of 1600 BC for the eruption precedes the date of 1595 BC for the Hittite sack of Babylon too closely to be ignored.

Mursulis I abandoned Babylon as soon as he had removed the city's treasures. This is notable. While the sack of a major urban center makes interesting reading in history books, it does the conqueror little good unless he follows up by consolidating political and economic power. Otherwise, no matter how rich the prize, he will receive only a one time infusion of capital. In order to maintain his military, his power and his empire he needs a steady stream of revenue. Mursulis I's decision not to follow up on his success at Babylon suggests there was no revenue to be had. This is the first indication we see that the aftermath of the Santorini eruption might have been felt far to the east.

In the vacuum left by the Hittite withdrawal, power in Babylon was assumed first by local Sumerians and then by the Kassites, a people from modern day Iran. It is not known whether Mursulis I planned further forays to the east. He was assassinated by ambitious members of his family upon his return from Babylon. In the longer term it didn't matter. The aftermath of the Santorini eruption had set in motion events that would alter the history of Anatolia, Syria and Canaan for centuries to come.

Recovery from the physical devastation of tsunami and the agricultural devastation of volcanic winter would have presented a daunting task for the kingdoms of the Eastern Mediterranean. Coastal infrastructure would have to be rebuilt from scratch. Materials would have to be bought. Workmen and crafts people paid and fed. None of that could even be attempted until the stratospheric sulfate aerosol veil had dissipated enough to make agriculture and animal husbandry viable again. Modern experience with volcanic winter suggests this would have taken at least a year.

In the wake of volcanic winter civilizations would have faced challenges beyond rebuilding physical infrastructure and re-establishing agriculture and commerce. Populations would have dwindled under the pressures of starvation and emigration. Those remaining would have lost confidence in both their government and their gods. Scarcity of resources would have exacerbated competition. Riots and insurrection were likely. Armies would have been forced to abandon expansion to maintain internal security. In the wake of the Santorini eruption civilizations would have struggled to hold their cultures together.

The Hittites were less exposed. They had less in the way of infrastructure based and agricultural economy. Their power was military and, when they chose to use it, diplomatic. Even so their flexibility was limited. They were parasitic rather than productive. Their prosperity waxed and waned with that of the economies they preyed upon. In the absence of new conquests or alliances the Hittites would be at the mercy of the prevailing economic situation. There is no record of any major Hittite forays in the century following Mursulis I's sack of Babylon. The *Edict of Telepinus* speaks of a kingdom in transition.

A period of internal turmoil followed the death of Mursulis I. Fratricide became the route to power. Eventually the Hittite nobility became disenchanted with the situation. The absolute power of the monarchy was curbed and a more tractable form of government put in place around 1500 BC.

In the Hittite New Kingdom, beginning about 1450 BC, chariot armies swept out of the Taurus Mountains and seized control of the Hurrian kingdom of Mitanni to the east, Syria to the south and Arzawa, comprising a good portion of Anatolia, to the west. Eventually the Hittite kings would live up to their Biblical billing as enemies of Egypt. They would pit their military might against the armies of the Pharaohs when the ambitions of the two empires collided in what is now southern Syria.

The Hittites enjoyed two centuries of power and prosperity. In time the pressures of the Egyptians from the south, the Assyrians from the east, the Kaska from the north and numerous internal revolts weakened the empire. Its last vestiges fell to yet another beneficiary of the Santorini eruption.

MEN OF BRONZE

At the time of the Santorini eruption the nearby mainland of Greece was dominated by a people known to modern scholars as Mycenaeans. The name is taken from the city of Mycenae, familiar to modern readers as the home of Agamemnon, leader of the forces attacking Troy in Homer's *Iliad*. We have no contemporary documents that reveal what the Mycenaeans called themselves. In Homer the attackers of Troy are most commonly referred to as Achaeans. They are never referred to as Greeks (Grakoi), implying that they were a civilization distinct from the Greek population of Homer's time, thought to be the Eighth Century BC. The contemporary Hittites referred to them as the Ahhiyawa. For convenience we will use the modern term Mycenaean.

Scholars have not been fortunate enough to find a historical record set down by the Mycenaeans, if indeed one ever existed. They were a literate society. They excelled at book keeping and maintained detailed administrative records, so we do have some contemporary writing on which to base an understanding of their civilization. Their medium of writing was soft clay tablets, which were presumably erased and re-used, something on the order of an ancient Etch-a-Sketch. The Mycenaean tablets on which writing survived were baked into permanence by fires that destroyed the cities, primarily Pylos and Knossos, where the records were kept.

We also have references in the extensive Hittite archive which allow us to draw some conclusions about the Mycenaeans and their place in the ancient world. In fact, it is a unique Hittite document that establishes the Mycenaeans as a cohesive empire rather than a collection of cities ruled by individual kings. In this document, dated from around 1225 BC, a Hittite king lists those rulers he views as great kings, a term used at the time for rulers over other kings. In modern terms a ruler over other rulers is an emperor. The king of the Ahhiyawa is included in the Hittite list, and then conspicuously lined out. This presumably means that the Mycenaeans were regarded by their peers as an empire up until that time, but degenerated into what appears to be a confederation of independent city-states.

Perhaps the most telling historical reference comes from the Fifth Century BC historian Herodotus, who writes of men of bronze who sold their fighting skills to the Pharaohs of Egypt. Egyptian military annals corroborate the wide use of mercenary forces, particularly in the conflicts waged during the Egyptian New Kingdom. This indicates that the Mycenaeans committed at least some part of their younger male population to overseas warfare. This had two benefits. It provided income for the rulers and cleared potential troublemakers out of the political system.

The Mycenaeans are thought to have originated from Western Anatolia. Their DNA shows a high frequency of the Anatolian haplogroup J2a-M410, also noted in many Minoan remains. A notable feature of their architecture was the megaron, a building in which a central courtyard has four supporting columns at its corners. This feature has been excavated in Anatolia, the earliest examples dating from around 2500 BC. An additional common feature is the burial of important members of the Mycenaean and Anatolian societies in shaft graves.

The arrival of the Mycenaean's predecessors on mainland Greece appears to have been inauspicious. Archaeologists searching for the roots of civilization in a specific area begin with a search for breaks in cultural continuity. The population and culture of mainland Greece were remarkably stable during the early years of the Bronze Age, beginning around 3200 BC. People lived in small, relatively isolated villages, much as they had during the preceding Neolithic Age.

The situation changed around 2300 BC. A large growth in population indicated an influx of outsiders. A number of villages showed signs of destruction and rebuilding, with different styles of dwellings, pottery and tools that spoke of a change in culture and technology. The migration brought a period of apparent poverty, with the same land supporting a greater population and no increase in resources to be distributed among them. Metals were in short supply. The commonality of housing in villages suggests little social stratification. Compared with nearby contemporary societies in the Minoan Islands, Anatolia or Canaan, and the more distant cultures in Egypt and Sumer, mainland Greece was a backwater.

The economic situation on mainland Greece evolved over time. Larger buildings began to appear, including a palace style structure at Marathon and a megaron at Thebes. It is difficult to build a complete picture of any stage of Greek history from analysis of structures. Many major sites have been built over by successive generations into modern times. Excavation can occur only at random during modern redevelopment. Included in this group, and stretching back into the Mycenaean age, are the Greek capitol of Athens and the northern city of Iolkos, the legendary starting point for the voyage of Jason and the Argonauts. Sites that have not been rebuilt since Mycenaean times present their own issues. Many cities were built on rock and re-built during Mycenaean times, which meant the original structures were scraped away down to bedrock to accommodate new construction.

In addition to structures for the living are the grave sites that have been unearthed. Burials are unique archaeological finds. Absent looting, the dead are normally left to rest undisturbed. Surviving grave goods can provide clues to the wealth, as well as the economic and social organization, of a culture. Notable among finds in Greece are warrior burials from a time after 2300 BC but preceding 1600 BC, which is the date currently accepted by historians as the beginning of the Mycenaean era.

Two graves contained boars' tusk helmets, used sparingly by the elite of the warrior aristocracy of the later Mycenaeans. These helmets were special enough to merit mention in Homer's *Iliad*. The helmets are felt-lined headgear with about sixty boar's tusks sewn in place to protect the wearer. Light weight and effectiveness make the boars' tusk helmet a sophisticated leap in armor technology. The skill, time and resources needed to make just one such helmet suggest the growth of social stratification based on military prowess.

The burials from this period found to date have not been ostentatious. While there is some danger in reasoning from the absence of evidence, the norm in ancient societies was to send the fallen aristocracy to the afterlife with the trappings they enjoyed on Earth. Perhaps the best known example is the funerary treasure of the Egyptian Pharaoh Tutankamun, who was interred with a hoard of priceless items in addition to a disassembled war chariot and numerous edged weapons and sets of archery paraphernalia. The Greek burials show no locally made treasure and no spoils of conquest.

In fact Greece harbored little or nothing to conquer. The presence of sophisticated war fighting technology and the absence of wealth raises the question of how the technology was paid for. And if the technology was not being used to accumulate wealth, we are entitled to wonder what it was being used for.

Mycenaean civilization moved from evolution to transformation with the shaft grave period, beginning about 1600 BC and running until approximately 1450 BC. Quite abruptly the previously impoverished Greek mainland was awash in riches. Warriors are buried in funerary armor with gold death masks. The weapons buried with them are often inlaid with precious stones or intricate carvings of scenes from life. Women were buried in high gold crowns and clothing rich with gold ornaments. In one case, children were wrapped in gold foil for inhumation. Many of the grave goods contained items that could have only been imported from distant sources. The contrast is startling, and raises the question of how a culture grew so rich and so cosmopolitan so quickly.

The beginning of the Mycenaean shaft grave period occurring at the same time as the Santorini eruption cannot be dismissed as coincidence. In fact it addresses another issue that scholars have carefully ignored. The Minoans, whose civilization was shattered by the eruption appear, from all we have learned, not to have maintained a military establishment. That raises the question of how a peaceful people could hope to conduct regional commerce in a maritime environment infested with pirates.

The pirate threat was serious and long standing, persisting well past the Bronze Age. No less an historical figure than Julius Caesar was seized and held by pirates in his youth. Caesar's solution was to return at the head of a Roman military expedition and crucify his tormentors. The Minoans must have had a similar threat to hold over the heads of would-be freebooters if they were to operate a trading network.

Evidence of this threat can be seen in a wall decoration unearthed at Akrotiri. A group of armed warriors wearing Mycenaean style kilts and carrying Mycenaean style tower shields are clearly visible. This is not a picture of an attack against the city. There is no evidence of hostility on the part of the Mycenaeans. The likely conclusion is that warlike Mycenaeans had been recruited by the Minoans to provide security for their fleets and to mete out punishment to pirates who violated their commerce.

Seismic activity on Santorini prior to the eruption sent residents scrambling for sanctuary. The absence of human remains in Akrotiri establishes that the city was evacuated in advance of the eruption. We know from pictorial evidence that there was contact between the residents of Akrotiri and the Mycenaeans. Mainland Greece would be a logical refuge for evacuees. Prevailing west to east winds would have protected the mainland from significant impact from both particulate and stratospheric ejecta. No significant trace of Santorini ejecta has been found on mainland Greece.

An influx of Minoan refugees would explain the sudden wealth appearing in mainland Greece. It would also account for the arrival of the engineering skills necessary to construct Mycenaean cities and other works of infrastructure. Minoan commercial expertise could underlie the growth of trade during the shaft grave period. The similarity between Minoan Linear A writing and Mycenaean Linear B suggests that the Mycenaeans may have co-opted symbols from Minoan writing to render their own Greek language into written form.

This sort of marriage of convenience is not unheard of. An example can be found in France. Following the collapse of the Western Roman Empire in the Fifth Century AD portions of Gaul came under the rule of a barbarian group known as Merovingians. This was not the end of Roman presence in the area. In fact, the remaining Roman aristocrats controlled much of the economy and financed the barbarian kingdom. The two groups already had a long standing relationship. The barbarians had hired out their fighting skills serving as auxiliary forces in the Roman army. When the grave of the first Merovingian king was found, it was determined that he had been buried in the livery of a Roman officer. Street names in older parts of Paris suggest that Roman influence persisted into the Ninth Century AD. The Merovingians monopolized military power, but they were reliant on the engineering prowess and economic organization of the surviving Romans to provide the staples and comforts of civilization.

Similar synergy may have existed between the warlike Mycenaeans of mainland Greece and the cosmopolitan Minoans fleeing the effects of the Santorini eruption. The later Greek historian Thucydides asserts that the Minoans obtained a navy to deal with pirates. How the navy was obtained and how it was constituted is not mentioned. It might have consisted in whole or in part of Mycenaean mercenaries. Minoan wealth could explain the presence of expensive war fighting technology in the Mycenaean arsenal.

Minoan influence may also provide a clue to the unusual style of Mycenaean governance. Bronze Age empires normally functioned under a single ruler holding court in a single large capitol. The Mycenaeans employed a distribution of power in which individual kings held court in their own capitols, apparently with some form of allegiance to an overall ruler in one of the larger capitols, perhaps Mycenae. Mainland Greece is not large, certainly not by comparison with other empires of the era. The terrain is no more rugged than that of the Taurus Mountain stronghold of the Hittites. Difficulty of overland travel should not have been an obstacle to unification.

The Minoan model of governance was developed under a much different set of circumstances. Beyond the Mediterranean island of Crete, the Minoan empire was spread across numerous Aegean islands. The sea was a natural obstacle to unification. The location and topography of individual islands could impose unique requirements. A distributed governance model would best fit such a situation.

We have a wealth of written evidence detailing the organization and governance of Mycenaean city-states. The largest hoard comes from the city of Pylos, which was located on the southwest coast of mainland Greece. The occupants kept administrative and commercial records on soft clay tablets. Around 1190 BC the city burned to the ground, baking one year's worth of soft clay records into permanence.

At one time the city's destruction was thought to have come at the hands of seaborne raiders. The preserved tablets do establish that the city maintained a cadre of eighty coast watchers to warn of hostile approach by sea. However, Late Bronze Age warfare involved intensive use of projectile weapons, leaving any battlefield strewn with bronze arrowheads and lead sling bullets. No such concentration has been found at Pylos.

The absence of sling bullets is particularly telling. The ancient sling consisted of a leather pouch and two attached cords. It could be carried in an individual soldier's kit with minimal weight penalty. Ammunition could be issued as needed from stores or foraged locally. Modern tests with replicas suggest the centripetal acceleration achieved by whirling the sling could produce a projectile launch energy only slightly less than that of a .44 magnum revolver. In ancient times the resulting range of four hundred yards could be exceeded only by the composite recurve bow. This range would have been critical to seaborne raiders. Composite bows tended to delaminate with exposure to sea air, rendering them useless.

An inspection of the plan of Pylos deduced by archaeologists provides a more likely explanation for its destruction. Mycenaean governance involved highly centralized control at the city level, which left large quantities of valuable olive oil stored in a palace made largely of wood. Interior lighting would have involved open flames. Storage of masses of liquid accelerant in a flammable structure in close proximity to other flammable structures was a recipe for disaster. In short, Pylos was a firetrap. The extent of destruction should come as no surprise. The modern American cities of Chicago and Seattle both burned to the ground in the Nineteenth Century AD.

The Pylos fire may not have been entirely accidental. The destruction occurred during the dates (1194 BC to 1184 BC) given by the historian Eratosthenes for the Trojan War. Pylos sent a large contingent as part of the Achaean expeditionary force. The loss of experienced personnel may have resulted in hazardous storage. Additionally, later literary tradition holds that there was considerable internal turmoil in the city-states of mainland Greece while their kings were away. A coup attempt or local insurrection may have resulted, inadvertently or otherwise, in the fire.

The timing does raise one disturbing question about the validity of the Pylos record as a blueprint for Mycenaean society. The destruction of the city occurred after 1225 BC, the date at which the Hittite king struck the Mycenaean king from the list of rulers he considered his equal. Records of imperial administration and taxation may have been discontinued at that time, but the disintegration of the Mycenaean empire does not appear to have affected the organization of the component city-states. Limited hoards of tablets found in other cities and dating from before 1225 BC show a similar pattern of administration and commerce.

Mycenaean cities were ruled by a king, called a *wa-na-ka* in the syllabic parlance of Linear B. Often they were protected by what were called by later Greeks cyclopean walls, a reference to building stones that were so large only the mythical Cyclops could muster the strength to move them. This was an unintentional but accurate testament to Mycenaean engineering. Within the walls was a palace, generally an adaptation of the megaron style building, which served as reception hall, residence, religious shrine and storage vault for valuables. The construction materials appear from analysis of the remains to have been timbers for support with wood and various types of stone used for walls. Little of the old decoration survives. In its day it would have been colorful and ornate. Surrounding buildings provided quarters and administrative work space for members of the king's court. Additional buildings outside the main city walls also served the same purpose, as well as housing commercial enterprises.

Based on the Pylos tablets and other finds in Linear B script, society in the central city and the surrounding lands was rigidly stratified. Life was regulated by the king and his close associates. At the top of the social order were the king and the palace entourage, a group of officials and warriors. Directly beneath them and part of the palace were craft and trades people who worked directly for the king. They could be engaged in anything from textile work to chariot repair to the export of trade goods. They appear to have been free to engage in limited entrepreneurship. Next in the social order were a class of free citizens, many of whom worked farms or tended flocks outside the physical orbit of the palace but whose communal settlements were connected to the palace by a network of roads and bridges. They were supervised by one or more direct subordinates of the king. Apparently they were also free to engage in some level of entrepreneurship. Lowest in rank were slaves, presumably either taken in battle or purchased by barter.

The major Mycenaean cities could be quite large. Geophysical survey of Pylos indicates the total inhabited area at up to seventy five acres. The remains of a sophisticated water management system have been found, suggesting that a high population density could be supported within the city. Some evidence of fortification walls has been uncovered but Pylos, unlike Mycenae and some other cities, does not seem prepared to withstand siege. It may be that the terrain and the wide area controlled from the city were better suited to mobile defense involving maneuver forces. There is ample evidence of warlike nature at Pylos. Most or all of the fighting age male citizens were probably subject to some level of military levy, depending on how urgent the immediate need or how lucrative the available opportunity.

The Pylos tablets give us a detailed picture of the city's activities, down to the number of women working as bath attendants. They give no clue how Pylos fit into the overall scheme of Mycenaean civilization. There are no communications with other cities, although it is clear that the cities were part of an overall society. There is no indication of any feudal structure above the city level that would give us an idea of which city or king might have been pre-eminent. There are no diplomatic communications with other nation-states, although it is clear from the presence of trade goods that regular contact existed. There are none of the permanent records that would be necessary to maintain Pylos' bureaucracy for more than one year.

It may be that Linear B archival records were rendered on perishable material that would require less storage space. The climate of Greece is not conducive to preservation. We know of much of the writing in later alphabetic Greek only by reference. Even in the case of surviving examples like the *Iliad* and *Odyssey,* the copies we have are much later than the original writing. Alphabetic Greek letters first show up on bits of pottery from the Ninth Century BC. The oldest complete book we have was recovered in less than pristine condition from the funeral of a Macedonian noble dated to approximately 355 BC. The survival prospects of much older Mycenaean writing are questionable.

The absence of contemporary writing leaves us to rely on the tales of later Greeks for clues to the impact of Santorini on the Mycenaeans. The Eighth Century BC poet Hesiod describes a great battle between the chief god, Zeus, and a giant sea monster during which great waves battered the shore and earthquakes arose. This may have its roots in lore related to the Santorini eruption. The Fifth Century BC playwright Euripides, in his work *Hippolytus*, describes a great roar followed by a towering wave approaching the Saronic Gulf. The Saronic Gulf is on the southeast coast of mainland Greece, facing Santorini.

Mainland Greece suffered only from the tidal action raised by the Santorini eruption. There is no evidence of volcanic winter. The Mycenaeans were able to parlay their comparative good fortune into imperial stature. The collapse of their empire would play a pivotal role in the final chapter of the impact of the Santorini eruption on the Eastern Mediterranean.

RESOLUTION

The physical impact of the Santorini eruption in the Eastern Mediterranean was transitory. The last traces of ejecta would have settled out of the stratosphere within the space of no more than a few years. The return of temperatures normal to the region allowed agriculture and animal husbandry to flourish as before. Tidal damage to the trading infrastructure was repaired.

Life for the surviving population, however, would not be the same. The cataclysm destroyed the economic system that supported the prevailing political structure. The Minoans became more dependent on the Mycenaeans. The Hyksos could no longer maintain their grip on the Nile Delta. The patchwork of kingdoms in Anatolia and Syria became vulnerable. The result was profound political and cultural change that would prevail for centuries. The few cultures that benefitted from the cataclysm expanded at the expense of less fortunate domains. Power was concentrated and economies were integrated. Initially viable and prosperous, that new reality ultimately proved to be sown with the seeds of its own destruction.

The Santorini eruption left three nascent empires in its aftermath. Over the following centuries the Egyptians would expand farther southward into the gold-rich land of Nubia and northward into Canaan and Syria. The Hittites would conquer the Hurrian kingdom of Mittani to the east and add the agricultural wealth of numerous Anatolian kingdoms to their holdings in Syria. The Mycenaeans would consolidate mainland Greece and gain control of the Minoan trading complex, as well as expanding their own trade into Europe. Commercial enterprises prospered in the region during the Late Bronze Age. Trade routes and trading centers were protected from opportunistic monarchs and marauders by powerful imperial armies. The empires and their armies were in turn supported and expanded by taxes on the growing trade and flourishing agriculture.

The imperial armies of the Late Bronze Age were highly organized and technically sophisticated. Development of the composite recurve bow permitted accurate volume delivery of projectiles that could penetrate three fingers of copper shielding. Light, maneuverable chariots provided mobile platforms for archers, allowing projectile delivery capability to be massed at critical points on the field of battle. Large infantry forces were grouped into units under successively larger commands, permitting tailored deployment under effective operational control. Infantry strength was augmented by mercenary forces, often supplied to both the Egyptians and Hittites by the Mycenaeans.

Aside from excursions into coastal Anatolia, the Mycenaeans appear to have been content with their lucrative role as manufacturers, traders and mercenaries. The Hittites and the Egyptians focused considerable effort on imperial expansion. Whenever the situation permitted, the Hittites preferred spear-point diplomacy to actual fighting. They often left conquered ruling elites in place and couched their conquests in terms of alliances. This was effective only within limits. The Hittite army was called upon to put down numerous revolts. The Egyptians took a different approach to solidifying expansion. Children of the conquered elite were taken to Egypt to be raised according to Egyptian customs and then returned to rule as figureheads. This policy of Egyptianization also had limits. Imperial exploitation was no more popular in ancient times than it is today.

In addition to quelling internal rebellion, the Egyptian and Hittite empires were forced to defend their borders against outside incursion. Powerful neighbors viewed the wealth of the empires with envy. The Libyans to the west of Egypt had designs on the Nile Delta. Pharaohs who were not actually fighting bore considerable expense to fortify and garrison the border. The Assyrians to the east of the Hittites had suffered episodes of mistreatment. They were alert for any opportunity to settle accounts. Only force or the threat of force was enough to hold them at bay. Occupation and defense were a constant drain on Hittite resources.

The greatest threat to both empires was their expansion into the same area, the southern portion of modern Syria. Active hostilities ramped up beginning around 1308 BC, with the ascension of Pharaoh Seti I to the Egyptian throne. He mounted several expeditions to recover territory taken by the Hittites along their mutual and fluid border. The Hittites responded with military force. Hostilities came to a head in 1274 BC at the Syrian city of Kadesh.

The battle of Kadesh is the first military encounter in history for which we have any detailed narrative. The surviving narrative is Egyptian in origin and slanted accordingly, but the details it provides give us an appreciation of the scale of events that grew out of the Santorini eruption. They also offer insight into the forces that would eventually bring an end to the great empires.

The major players at Kadesh were the Egyptian Pharaoh Ramses II, son of Seti I, and the Hittite King Muwatallis. Ramses II came to power in 1279 BC and continued the campaigns of his father to recover territory taken by the Hittites. He committed an army of five divisions of infantry, four named after Egyptian gods and one Canaanite called the Na'arm Group. An Egyptian infantry division contained 5,000 soldiers, making a total of 25,000. Supporting chariot forces are estimated at between 2,500 and 3,500 vehicles, each with a driver and archer. Espionage was well established in the area. Muwatallis probably had a good estimate of the size of the Egyptian force. His own army, consisting of Hittite regular forces and those of allied kingdoms, amounted to an infantry strength of about 37,000 supported by 3,500 three man Hittite style chariots.

Ramses II's initial objective was Kadesh, a large city on the Orontes River. He marched his four Egyptian divisions north from the border garrison at Sile. The Na'arm group departed inland from the coast of Canaan. Based on later events, the plan appears to have been for the two forces to rendezvous to the north and west of Kadesh and from there mount an assault on the city.

According to the Egyptian narrative Muwatallis sent spies to Ramses II's camp to convince him the Hittite force was maneuvering well to the north of Kadesh when in fact they had already reached the city. Ramses II took the bait and pushed his forces northward into a trap. While this may have been the case, a more likely scenario is that Ramses II's actions were driven by his original scheme of maneuver. If the Egyptian divisions did not reach the city at the same time as the Na'arm group, his force would be split and at the mercy of the Hittites. Both the Egyptians and the Hittites had campaigned extensively in the area. Both would have known the route and timing of march from any location to any other. Rather than admit that his own complex battle plan had forced his hand, Ramses II may have constructed a fiction of Hittite duplicity to explain his actions.

Ramses II reached the rendezvous point north and west of Kadesh with his lead division unmolested. The Hittites struck while the second division in the line of march was executing a river crossing. Hittite chariot forces mauled the trapped division and turned on Ramses II and his lead division while the other two Egyptian divisions were still on the far side of the river and unable to come to his assistance. Ramses II's camp was overrun and abandoned. The Egyptian forces were saved only by the timely and almost certainly planned arrival of the Na'arm Group, and by a successful river crossing of the third of Ramses II's four Egyptian divisions. The Hittite chariot forces were defeated and pushed back to the city.

At this point the battle reached stalemate. Muwatallis had not yet committed any significant portion of his massive infantry strength to combat. Ramses II's chariot and infantry forces had sustained heavy casualties in defeating the Hittite chariot forces. An Egyptian assault against the intact Hittite infantry would have been suicidal. With his chariot forces shattered, Muwatallis was in no position to mount a counter-attack against the remaining Egyptians. Ramses II accepted his fate and returned to Egypt to mount a propaganda campaign to paint his adventure at Kadesh in the best possible light.

The Hittites were less fortunate. Although they reversed earlier gains made by Seti I in Syria, their losses at Kadesh were certainly crippling. Chariot forces could not be replaced overnight. According to a surviving Hittite manual it took more than five months to train the horse team. In addition, new vehicles had to be constructed. Crews had to be recruited and trained in maneuver and tactics. All this had to be paid for from a tax base that could not be arbitrarily expanded to meet military need. The process would have been slow and may have contributed to a debacle on the eastern flank of the Hittite Empire. In 1263 BC Assyrian forces under Shalmaneser I overran the Hittite vassal kingdom of Mitanni.

Ramses II had his own issues to contend with. Following the potentially embarrassing stalemate at Kadesh he undertook an extensive propaganda program involving infrastructure and monument building to salvage his reputation. Much of that was paid for with gold extracted from mines in Nubia. The Nubians were predictably upset by this larceny and multiple campaigns were required to quell unrest. Ramses II also had to garrison the western border against Libyan incursion.

It became clear to both the Egyptians and the Hittites that the cost of continued mutual hostilities endangered not only their borders but the existence of their empires. In 1258 BC the two empires concluded the earliest known written peace treaty. The impact of this treaty went beyond the former combatants. The military expenses of the Egyptians in particular and to some extent the Hittites, included the payment of Mycenaean mercenaries. Unbearable expense to the Egyptians and the Hittites was essential revenue to the Mycenaeans.

Economies of scale probably dictated that Mycenaean city-states provide mercenaries in organized groups. Prior to the introduction of coinage, payment would have been made to the ruler of the city-state in the form of shipments of grain. This is nowhere documented, but grain was the wealth of Egypt. Egyptian officials were paid according to a salary scale stated in quantities of grain. There is no reason contract mercenaries would not be compensated in the same way. This arrangement had an additional advantage. The families of individual mercenaries remained at home as de-facto hostages against privateering.

The mercenaries would presumably share in the wealth accumulated by their families upon their return from service. The rulers of the Mycenaean city-states would gain a source of staple food that was not reliant on local agriculture. They could then repurpose portions of their population to manufacturing, such as pottery and textiles, and to trade and other lucrative activities.

The loss of this revenue and the related outlet for the energies of ambitious younger Mycenaeans appears to have had an immediate effect. Around 1250 BC several Mycenaean cites showed signs of reinforced fortification. In the absence of an external threat, the most probable cause was the potential uprising of restive elements within their own society. Later Greek myth and drama, for example Homer's *Odyssey* and Sophocles' *Orestia,* present this type of unrest in Mycenaean Greece as major themes. It is unlikely to have simply been invented. Previously mentioned Hittite documentation indicates a complete breakdown of the Mycenaean Empire in 1225 BC.

No surviving Mycenaean writing addressed either the empire or its collapse. Later dramatic writing coupled with contemporary documentation from other sources gives us a picture of what happened. Hittite correspondence indicates that the Assyrians had pressed their advantage and forced open a route through the Hittite empire to the Mediterranean Sea. The Hittite king concluded a treaty that called for prevention of contact between the Mycenaeans and the Assyrians. This reduced the commercial opportunities of the Mycenaeans, and may have been the motivation for exploration into the Black Sea region, as dramatized in the later *Voyage of Argo.*

Whatever commercial expansion was achieved was insufficient. A following military initiative fared even worse. Groups of Mycenaeans allied themselves with the King of Libya in an attempt to overrun the Nile Delta and seize the agricultural riches of Egypt. The result was catastrophic. The Libyan and Mycenaean forces were organized largely along infantry lines. The chariot army of Pharaoh Merneptah inflicted heavy casualties and drove them from the field.

A note on this and later battles is in order. Egyptian records, and history is invariably written by the victors, relate that the Libya's allies came from the sea. This has led to the unnecessary and unwarranted invention of a mysterious 'Sea People', who came from no known source and raided extensively in the Eastern Mediterranean. The term was coined not by the Egyptians, but by a European Egyptologist in the Nineteenth Century AD.

The Egyptians provided a detailed catalog of the areas devastated by the later-named Sea People. Included were the island of Cyprus and much of Anatolia. Excluded were *Tanaj* and *Keftu,* the Egyptian names for the Greek mainland and the island of Crete. Later Greek drama makes no mention of any assault on Greek lands or islands by an external enemy. The implication is clear. The so-called Sea People were in fact elements of the former Mycenaean Empire. As we will see later in this chapter, identification of the Sea People as Mycenaean is supported by archaeological finds.

Failure to overrun Egypt in alliance with the Libyans was a setback. It was not the end of Mycenaean desperation. Or opportunity. Another lucrative target was developing to the east. The Hittite Empire was failing, leaving vassal states long dependent on the protection of the imperial army open to plunder. The initial phase of the Mycenaean invasion has come down to us as the story of the Trojan War. A summary of the epic poem *Cipria,* which preceded the events of Homer's *Iliad* in time, paints a picture of a fragmented Mycenaean Empire ruled as city-states pulled together under the leadership of one of their kings, Agamemnon, to attack the city of Troy.

The city is not called Troy in the poems of the epic cycle. It is Ilios, a name now thought to correspond to the Hittite city-state of Wilusa. Wilusa had been a bone of contention for more than half a century. Homer's *Iliad* mentions prior hostilities. The Hittite *Tawagalawa Letter,* dated to around 1250 BC, refers to the end of a war between the Hittites and the Mycenaeans over the city. By 1205 BC the Assuwa, a confederation of city-states, had seceded from the failing Hittite empire and gained control of the Aegean coast of Anatolia. Without the threat of a Hittite imperial army, Anatolia was open to invasion.

The Mycenaean force of more than 50,000 men borne on a fleet of more than 1,100 ships was equal to or greater in size than the forces launched by the Hittites and Egyptians only eighty years earlier in 1274 BC with the intention of expanding their empires. The Mycenaeans clearly had their sights set on more than a single city. The Hittites and Egyptians met at Kadesh. The Mycenaeans and the remains of the Hittite city-states in Anatolia met at Wilusa.

The fall of Wilusa around 1184 BC opened the gates for the Mycenaean forces to raid their way down the coasts of Syria and Canaan. The major port of Ugarit fell to siege sometime after 1192 BC. As previously discussed, surviving documentation allows us to closely approximate this date with confidence. The city's destruction establishes that the objective of the Mycenaeans during this phase of their foray was plunder rather than conquest and occupation. Referring again to Homer's *Odyssey,* Menelaus, the king of Sparta, boasts of taking treasure from foreign speaking peoples in the Egyptian lands (probably Canaan). The Egyptian catalog of the lands plundered ranges from the Island of Cyprus all the way across the former Hittite Empire.

Egypt was the ultimate objective of the Mycenaean invasion. The Nile was the breadbasket of the Eastern Mediterranean. Its capture would secure the future of the Mycenaeans. Organized, aggressive and flush with more than fifteen years of victories, they launched a two pronged assault against the Egyptians, one by land and one by sea. The beating the Mycenaean-Libyan alliance had taken at the hands of Pharaoh Merneptah was a shadow of the defeat inflicted on the Mycenaeans by the successor Pharaoh Ramses III.

The seaborne Mycenaean assault used ships that were fitted out for the transport of infantry, not for naval combat. Long exposure to salt water tended to delaminate the powerful composite bows of the time, so the most potent projectile weapons were not available to the Mycenaeans. Reference to Homer's *Odyssey* shows Odysseus leaving his most powerful bow behind when he departed by sea to fight at Troy. The Egyptians were able to use composite bows from shore positions. Due to the short term exposure on ships operating close to the coast, they were also able to use them from the specially built fighting castles of their vessels. Pictorial representations of the sea battle survive, but little is known of the land battle beyond the outcome. As in the Libyan offensive, the Mycenaeans relied heavily on infantry. Again this proved no match for the Egyptian chariot forces.

The failure of the Mycenaean assault on Egypt left the remnants of the former empire shattered and scattered. Egyptian tax rolls show that they settled some, known as Sherden, throughout the 42 nomes of Egypt. The Sherden had a long history with the Egyptians. At one time they had harassed the coast of Canaan as pirates. At another they had fought as mercenaries in the service of the Pharaoh. This familiarity may have played a role in their treatment. It does serve to illustrate the complex interrelationship among the empires.

Another group called the Peleset was cited in the *Harris Papyrus* as being resettled in Canaan. As previously discussed, they are better known through Judeo-Christian scripture as the Philistines. Others remained as occupants of portions of the former Hittite Empire. The Tjekker are mentioned in an Egyptian document as controlling the Eastern Mediterranean port of Dor. Some settled on the Island of Cyprus, while others apparently returned to mainland Greece.

Archaeological finds on Cyprus and in the five Philistine cities, in particular pottery and loom weights, establish that the people were definitely Mycenaean in origin. In the case of the Philistines, this conclusion is reinforced by the architectural style found in their cities. Although individual Mycenaean elements survived for a time in various locations, and some may have briefly prospered, there would never again be a Mycenaean empire. Nor even an alliance. In time Mycenaean culture would wither and die, taking with it the Minoans, whom they had by then absorbed.

The Santorini eruption of 1600 BC upset the existing order in the Eastern Mediterranean and created conditions for the rise of three great empires. The region, constricted by hostile neighboring kingdoms, was not large enough to support the ambitions and requirements of all three. The Hittites, weakened by external military pressure and internal friction, eventually could not defend themselves against the remnants of a Mycenaean Empire made desperate by shrinking economic opportunities. They retreated into a few neo-Hittite enclaves and eventually faded away. History would not acknowledge their achievements for more than two thousand years.

The success of the Mycenaeans was short-lived. They fell prey to their own ambitions and to the power of the Egyptian military. The Egyptians, for their part, had withdrawn from Canaan by 1160 BC and left a proxy force of Philistines to insure against any rise of a Canaanite power. Only defense of the homeland and the adjacent Nubian provinces remained. Ramses III, last of the imperial Pharaohs, was murdered in a harem coup in 1155 BC.

The collapse of the Eastern Mediterranean Bronze Age empires brought changes that would not fully mature for centuries. Nascent forms of alphabetic writing, born in Egypt, took root in Canaan. From there the concept would first ride Phoenician trading ships to Greece, and then expand throughout the western world. Citizens of Greece, freed from the shackles of empire, began the long process of wresting the destiny of humankind from tyrants. Beyond the Eastern Mediterranean other scenarios were unfolding.

SIN CITY

The name Babylon has long been synonymous with decadent urban lifestyle. As with any stereotype there is some kernel of underlying truth, but pejorative connotations were only a footnote to the greatness of the ancient city on the Euphrates. It was the first metropolis. A vibrant center of commerce and administration. A cradle of learning where sophisticated mathematics and astronomy were developed and practiced.

The city's reputation was such that early historians wrote glowingly of it. The Third Century BC Greek engineer Philo included the Hanging Gardens of Babylon on a list that became enshrined as the Seven Wonders of the World. It was a case of the city's reputation growing so luminous that it outshone reality. No trace of any hanging gardens has been found in Babylon. They are currently thought to have been located in the city of Nineveh.

Babylon was the culmination of a trend toward urbanization begun in Mesopotamia by the Sumerians sometime before 3,000 BC. The name Mesopotamia comes from Greek, meaning in the middle of the rivers. Rather than being bordered by the Tigris and Euphrates, Mesopotamia can better be thought of as approximating modern Iraq. Who the Sumerians were and how they got there Remain unresolved questions. The Sumerian language is unlike any other in the area. Its source is unknown.

A great deal is known about the Sumerians during their tenure in Mesopotamia. Beginning around 3,000 BC they developed a system of writing we now call cuneiform, after the wedge shape of the characters. The characters were formed with a stylus on tablets of soft clay, which were then baked into permanence. Sumerian tablets have survived in the hundreds of thousands. Those that have been translated provide insight into politics, medicine, religion, commerce and daily life. The Sumerian language died out eventually, but cuneiform was adaptable enough to survive in Akkadian and Hittite among other languages. Also surviving are the remains of the Sumerians' other contribution to civilization, the urban center used as a seat of organization and administration.

Modern understanding of Sumerian civilization is fairly recent. At the outset of the Nineteenth Century AD the remains of the ancient cities of Mesopotamia existed only as great mounds of sand in the deserts of the Ottoman Empire, abandoned by the shifting courses of the rivers that had once given them life. The European powers, primarily England, France and Germany, began to see the mounds as sources of prestige-enhancing museum exhibits after finely crafted statues and tablets full of strange writing had been found and sold by local Arabs.

Expeditions descended in a flurry of what can best be described as smash and grab archaeology. Trenches were dug down through the mounds to recover artifacts, with mounds of resulting tailings left behind. Little attention was paid to the context of the finds. This activity has been much criticized, but without it the energy and investment devoted to discovery might have been channeled elsewhere and a critical chapter in the history of humankind left buried under the sand. As the century progressed, tablets were translated and archaeological techniques refined. The story of the ancient cities began to emerge.

A city can be defined as a large, permanent, organized human habitation. How they got started is debated by scholars. Early clusters of permanent structures have been found in Southern Turkey and at Eridu in southernmost Iraq, sometimes referred to as the Mesopotamian Garden of Eden. These appear to be religious shrines rather than large scale permanent domicile. Other early locations, specifically Catal Hoyuk in Anatolia and Jericho in Canaan, are clearly organized for human habitation, with structural provision for housing and for security against the forces of nature, predatory animals and aggressive neighbors.

The cities of the Sumerians took the concept a step farther. Unlike the northern areas around the Tigris and Euphrates Rivers, the southern reaches of the Rivers have no surrounding mountains to produce the rainfall associated with agricultural fertility. The Sumerian farmers' answer was irrigation. They built intricate systems of dykes and canals to bring the waters of the great rivers to their crops. The rivers were unpredictable and the irrigation systems were accordingly maintenance intensive. This gave rise to a bureaucracy to organize and administer the work. Sumerian cities grew initially as centers of irrigation systems.

Land fed by regular irrigation can produce more per unit of area than land dependent on irregular rainfall for fertility. That allowed the Sumerians' lands to support large non-agricultural urban populations. Specialized crafts were developed. Medical practice was organized and laws were codified. Agriculture was supplemented by other productive ventures such as manufacture and commerce. The wealth of cities grew in disproportion to simple farm output.

The oldest Mesopotamian city is Uruk, home of the legendary Gilgamesh. It is a vast site that has not been fully excavated. Some of the exploratory work done amounted to little more than treasure hunting. Later efforts focused primarily on the many levels of impressive architecture. At the height of its power the city was enclosed by five miles of defensive wall reputed to rise up to twenty feet high.

It first emerged as a city, rather than a simple settlement, around 3800 BC. It was an administrative center with wide ranging trade, as evidenced by a wealth of cylinder seals and tablets. The tablets do not contain writing as we know it, but rather a set of pictorial representations. These have been seen as precursors of actual writing. This may be denying them their due. Written representation of a single language may not have been of much use to a city trading with multiple cultures employing multiple languages. Pictures with obvious and universal meaning may have been a more effective medium of communication.

Cuneiform representation of the Sumerian language dates to around 3000 BC. The contents of the surviving tablets range from commercial and administrative records to school books and pharmaceutical formulae. Some of them appear to be literary in nature. Rather than actual narratives that can be readily understood today they seem to be reminders of oral traditions that would have been known to the Sumerian readers.

Modern scholars have tended to separate writing and oral tradition. An example is the Greek tales of the Trojan War. Historians have suggested the poems were passed down on an entirely oral basis by generations of bards until Homer committed them to writing. This is speculation based solely on an absence of writing. The Sumerian cuneiform tablets suggest such speculation may be without foundation. Oral tradition and writing appear to have been complementary.

Contemporary writing provides us with much of what we know about the early history of Mesopotamian civilization. Notable in the writing of the third millennium BC is the rise of the institution of kingship. Cities as administrative centers morphed into city-states, existing in a loose commercial confederation but often engaged in military conflict with one another for supremacy. The most strategically positioned of these city-states was Kish, located where the Tigris and Euphrates came closest to one another.

In 2340 BC ambitious leader named Sargon ascended to the kingship of Kish. His path to power is murky. He claimed royal blood through his mother, an unnamed priestess, and declared that he rose because he had found favor with the Goddess Ishtar.

Sargon's ambitions were not limited to the kingdom of Kish. He conquered the kingdom of Uruk as a starting point on his way to building what became known as the Akkadian empire. By Sargon's count his army prevailed in thirty four battles. He stretched his domain from the Persian Gulf in the south to the Taurus Mountains in the north, from the Mediterranean Sea in the west to the frontiers of what is now Iran in the east. City-states that had alternately confederated and quarreled were now under a single ruler. Akkadian administrators replaced local elites. Akkadian became the language of the empire.

Sargon built an entirely new type of city, Akkad, as his capitol. The location has eluded archaeologists, but we have a description from the later literary work *The Curse of Agade*. It describes a port facility and trading center with no agricultural underpinnings and no specific religious center. Akkad was constructed as the center of an empire, a city dependent entirely on commercial contact with the outside world for its economic survival. A city little different from the major cities of today.

The Akkadian Empire had built-in lines of fracture. Ambitious elites in the conquered cities were upset at being replaced. Outside nomadic and semi-nomadic forces saw rich pickings if successful raids could be mounted. Sargon's successors fought numerous campaigns to hold the empire together, but by 2200 BC it had disintegrated into the fractious conglomeration of city-states from which it had been constructed.

Archaeological evidence of the influence of the Akkadian empire is not as great as it might be if a massive building campaign had been undertaken in conjunction with its rise. There are some monuments testifying to its reach. Limited evidence does exist that Sargon's grandson penetrated into Anatolia during his reign. Contemporary and later writing suggests broad geographical scope, although some scholars question whether this may include propaganda that exaggerated the reach and impact of the Akkadian expansion. The fact that Akkadian persisted for the next thousand years as the commercial and diplomatic language of the Eastern Mediterranean should put any doubt as to the overall impact of the empire to rest.

Akkadian is a Semitic language, related to Arabic, Aramaic and Hebrew. Scholars have suggested that the Akkadians were a northern Semitic race proportionally more dependent on animal husbandry than agriculture, and that they conquered the more agriculturally oriented southern Sumerians in a contest over the use of land. No firm evidence either supports or eliminates this theory. More important is the fact that the cultures were bound together by a network of commerce essential for everyone's prosperity. Life went on no matter who claimed the mantle of the old Akkadian Empire. The last credible claimant to do so, the Sumerian kingdom of Ur, collapsed in 2053 BC, an event both predicted and dated by a lunar eclipse.

Anchored dates are essential in creating a Mesopotamian chronology. There is a surviving Sumerian king list, but it is clearly flawed. It begins with kings who ruled for tens of thousands of years each before the Great

Flood. Subsequent listings show a total of more years of reign by the listed kings than the calendar years that had elapsed during the stated time frame. The king list places the collapse of the Ur dynasty at 2006 BC. That is at odds by almost fifty years with the best available astronomical anchor we have.

While precise timing is not available, reliable records from the post-Akkadian period do allow us to gain a general understanding of events. We are concerned with two events. The movement of a people called the Amorites into Mesopotamia, and a change in the course of the Euphrates River to the point where it cut a channel near an insignificant village we now call Babylon.

The Amorites were people from Eastern Syria and Canaan who migrated eastward in sufficient strength to, over a period of time, gain control of Northern Mesopotamia. The precise boundaries of their domain shifted with the passage of years, but their influence was far-reaching. They controlled the Assyrian city of Ashur, which we know from the *Kultepe Texts* was a clearing house for tin from Afghanistan and silver from the Taurus Mountains. Their trading center, Kanesh (the Hittite Nesa) in Anatolia, was a two month trip by pack train. They traded from Aleppo in Syria to the Persian Gulf in the south of Mesopotamia.

Among the cities under Amorite control was Babylon, which was undergoing substantial growth due to its favorable location on the Euphrates. The control mechanism was for Amorite rulers to appoint vassal overlords in each of their cities. One of the most powerful of these rulers appointed the now-famous Hammurabi as his vassal to rule Babylon.

Hammurabi is known today as a conqueror and law-giver. While he was both, his main tools in the accumulation of power were politics and diplomacy. He forged alliances where he could, usurped power where possible and resorted to military force when necessary. The result is what we now call the Babylonian Old Kingdom. Little is known of the actual city during this period. The Euphrates changed course again in later years and submerged the old city. It will likely remain so for however many more years it takes the River change course again.

We have a copy of the laws of Hammurabi only because Babylon was later sacked by the Elamites and the Stela containing the laws taken to the city of Susa in Southern Iran. Archaeologists found it there some two thousand years later. Babylonian mathematics and astronomical observations survive on scattered tablets. Some of these suggest surprising sophistication. In one case the cycle of the planet Jupiter is measured by the area under a curve. This corresponds to the modern concept of integral calculus.

The Babylonian Old Kingdom had a fairly short life span, lasting only through five rulers. The last of the line perished, or at least vanished from the record, with the Hittite sack of the city in 1595 BC. Since this date is critical in matching events to the Santorini eruption, we need to understand how it is anchored.

The date comes from something called the Babylonian long chronology. This is one of four chronologies proposed for the period. The chronologies are derived from Second Millennium BC observations of the heliacal rising and setting of the planet Venus. The term heliacal rising has its roots in Helios, the Greek word for the sun. The heliacal rising of a planet is its initial rising after it was invisible due to its position relative to the sun. The heliacal setting is its final setting before it once again becomes invisible.

Tablets recording one set of observations correspond with the eighth year of the reign of Ammisaduqa, a successor of Hammurabi. The challenge in this methodology lies in matching a repeating astronomical cycle with a specific year of observation. Four possible dates might correspond with the recorded observations, and are the bases for four chronologies. Mathematical analysis (Huber) assigns a ninety nine percent probability that the long chronology is correct, and that the reign of Ammisduqa began in 1702 BC. From there we can use the lengths of reign assigned to the remaining kings to establish a date of 1595 BC for the final year of the last ruler of the Babylonian Old Kingdom.

It is usually assumed that the Hittites were able to sack Babylon as a result of weakness in the city's ruling structure. The Babylonian Old Kingdom reached its height under the rule of its founder, Hammurabi. Following his death, and the resulting loss of his diplomatic, military and administrative skills, subsequent rulers faced increasing pressures that resulted in a gradual dwindling of the span of their influence and power. This process is seen as culminating in the success of the Hittite expedition, and the subsequent takeover of the city by the Kassites.

This assumption fails to take account of the broader overall situation. The details of the Hittite movement from Hattusas to Babylon are not known, but it is clear that Mursulis I had to move a large, hostile expeditionary force through five hundred miles of Amorite controlled territory to sack an Amorite city. The failure of the Amorites to put up effective resistance at any point along the route of march suggests a systematic weakness in the ruling culture that went far beyond the city of Babylon. Amorite weakness by itself is not enough to explain the situation. If the Hittites found themselves unopposed, they would be free to sack other cities along the route of march as well. No record of this exists. The actions of the Hittites do make sense if the aftermath of the Santorini eruption had rendered the line of march destitute to the point where the benefits of victory were insufficient to justify the cost of assault.

Further complicating the scenario is the Kassite takeover of Babylon following the Hittite departure. It reinforces the question of why the Hittites were content to merely sack the city rather than seize power in the absence of Amorite strength. The Kassite takeover did not happen immediately. There is evidence of brief Sumerian rule before the Kassites assumed power. Neither the Kassite nor the Sumerian culture was Amorite.

The Kassites had previously attempted a military takeover of Babylonian territory. They were soundly defeated. For them to seize Babylon after 1595 BC, in the face of Sumerian opposition, implies a simultaneous collapse of both Amorite and Sumerian power. Very few events could have produced such a collapse. The leading candidate at time was an economic failure of a scope and scale consistent with the after-effects of the Santorini eruption. A failure that rendered Babylon worthless to the Hittites except as a one-time source of plunder, and that left a power vacuum in the area that no one was able to fill until the Kassites rose to prominence by default.

Surprisingly little is known about the Kassites, considering that they were able to conquer Sumeria in the wake of their takeover of Babylon and rule for more than four hundred years. They appear to be opportunistic raiders based in what is now Western Iran. They spoke a language that does not fit any current classification. Little of their writing has survived. We do not have the vocabulary necessary to make sense of what remains.

What we know of the Kassites comes from the writing of people they conquered or administered. Much of their success may be due to the fact that they adopted the civilization of Babylon rather than trying to replace it. It is tempting to think of them as barbarians aspiring to a loftier culture, but we simply don't know. What is apparent is that the Santorini eruption brought what we today would call regime change, without corresponding cultural change.

It is the power vacuum that permitted the rise of the Kassite kingdom rather than the Kassites themselves that points to the impact of the Santorini eruption. In the long term the effect was minimal. The Kassites continued the traditions and policies of the Babylonians. The commercial network administered from the great city rebuilt itself, albeit with a new cast of characters. Perhaps most important, the city continued as a center of learning and a repository of knowledge that today forms part of the legacy of the Santorini eruption.

No volcanic eruption, no matter how powerful, can, by itself, dictate the course of history. It can only act on existing civilizations to force them to adapt to new realities.

Before we take our next step forward in the examination of the impact of the Santorini eruption, we need to take a step back in both time and geography to understand a massive cultural shift that occurred in Europe and Western Asia. A shift that determined the state of civilization there at the time of the Santorini eruption.

THE ICEMAN COMETH

In order to pursue our exploration of the impact of the Santorini eruption beyond the Eastern Mediterranean and the adjoining lands of Mesopotamia, we will need to understand something of the surrounding world and the people who occupied it. Blind luck has given us a remarkable starting point. In 1991 AD hikers stumbled on human remains at an altitude of 10,500 feet in the Otzal Alps, on the border between Austria and Italy. Closer examination revealed that the discovery was a natural mummy. Radiocarbon analysis established that it had lain entombed in the ice for 5,300 years. The mummy was nicknamed Otzi, for the location where it was found. It is more commonly known as the Iceman.

Physical and scientific analysis determined the Iceman was a brown-eyed, arthritic, lactose intolerant male Caucasian. He was in his mid to late forties at the time of his death. At five feet, two inches, his height was on the low side of average for the descendants of the farmers who had migrated into Europe centuries before. He was dressed for mountain travel in a cloak of woven grass rather than animal fur. His shoes were a complex construction. The soles were bear hide and the uppers deerskin. They were stuffed with hay for warmth and held together by cords of bark. He carried equipment ranging from fire starting implements to tools and weapons to medical items that included wound dressings with a natural antibiotic and an assortment of natural pharmaceuticals. Tattoos on his body indicate that he belonged to an ordered society with established traditions.

We have no direct knowledge of the social structure in the region during The Iceman's lifetime. The fact that he carried a copper axe has been taken to mean that he enjoyed high status. That is questionable. There is no register of the socioeconomic distribution of copper items from that time and location. The inference also runs counter to the habit of higher status individuals to distance themselves from tools and rely on ornamentation to serve notice of their position. The absence of evidence of a retinue suggests that the Iceman did not occupy a leadership role. It seems more likely that he was a representative member of his society. The purpose of his final journey is a matter of speculation.

The Iceman died as a victim of homicide. A computed tomography scan identified an arrow head that had entered from behind and severed a major artery in his thoracic cavity. Such a wound would have resulted in rapid death from exsanguination. The motive for his death is unknown. Ritual murder, common in some ancient societies, is unlikely. A victim selected for such a fate would not have been carrying a full complement of travel items. A full stomach and the direction of the wound raise the likelihood that he was shot from ambush while resting after a large meal.

The fact that the body was not plundered is notable. There were items of both utility and value in the Iceman's personal kit. His assailant seems to have been bent on murder and nothing else. He may have refrained from robbery due to some social or religious stricture, or from fear of identification. We simply don't know. One conclusion that can be drawn is that the Iceman's contemporaries were skilled in the use of projectile weapons and prepared to employ those skills for homicidal purposes.

Prior to the discovery of the Iceman, our knowledge of Europe of 3300 BC had to be pieced together from analysis of relics, often fragments, discovered in random archaeological excavations. The perishables associated with everyday life have long since vanished. The context in which the surviving items are found is often degraded. Dating can be controversial, if not impossible. We are left with a patchwork of vague guesses and conflicting interpretations.

The Iceman provided an unprecedented look at a human of 3,300 BC, dressed and equipped as he was on the day he died, with his last meal still in his stomach. Importantly, he was found in the environment in which he lived. Variations in the quantities of isotopes of elements, primarily oxygen, strontium and iron, preserved in the enamel of human teeth can provide a picture of where someone grew up and spent his life. In the Iceman's case he likely grew up in the nearby Isarco River Valley and spent his adult years in the Venosta Valley, close to the place of his death. Pollen analysis places his death in the spring. It also allows us to trace the path that took him to the ten thousand foot glacier that preserved and eventually yielded his remains.

The Iceman's mummy is kept in a temperature and humidity controlled vault. Studies are conducted only rarely and planned with exacting care to maximize the knowledge recovered. No matter how comprehensive, analysis of the Iceman's remains still provides only a single snapshot through a very narrow window of time and geography. It can, however, be used in conjunction with other information to form some general extrapolations about the culture of Europe just before 3000 BC.

The Iceman's last meal consisted largely of cultivated cereal grains and the meat of a local wild goat known as an ibex. This, coupled with The Iceman's lactose intolerance, suggests a culture subsisting on farming, gathering and hunting, with no reliance on the milk of domesticated animals. The fact that the Iceman made his adult domicile close to the place where he grew up, both in fertile river valleys, reinforces the idea of an agricultural society tied to the land. Missing is the societal context. We do not know whether farming involved individual ownership, sharecropping, a feudal system or a system of rights to work common tribal ground.

The Iceman's last journey is also telling. His route took him toward an Alpine pass just west of the Similaun Glacier. The fact that an aging arthritic was attempting an Alpine crossing with no reserve food suggests a well travelled path with established rest stops and ample opportunities for re-provisioning. This in turn suggests that mobility had become sufficiently important to require routine penetration of the Alpine barrier between Italy and areas to the north.

The presence of a copper axe blade reveals the Iceman's culture was part of a wide ranging trade network. The presence of a variety of natural medicinal items among his possessions suggests a broad sharing of ideas and knowledge among contemporary cultures, as well as the organized maintenance of lore. This generally conforms to archaeological data from contemporary sites across Europe.

Archaeological remains are often more intriguing than informative. We know, for example, that development on Salisbury Plain in Britain that eventually became Stonehenge began around the time of the Iceman. Stonehenge is among the most studied and storied of all the ancient monuments. Its large stones have been traced to their quarry. Its astronomical orientation has been identified. Its surroundings have been excavated. Burials spanning fifteen centuries have been analyzed. We are still not certain of the full intent of its construction. We have little insight into the lives of the people who built it.

Claims of Druid origins can be dismissed. Druids were part of the later Iron Age Celtic culture. Activity on Salisbury Plain began during the Stone Age and ended during the Bronze Age. The site was active for fifteen hundred years. During that time it was under successive development by multiple cultures. We do not know why it was seen as important by so many for so long. Or why it was ultimately abandoned around the time of the Santorini eruption.

Items from all over Britain have been found on Salisbury Plain. This implies the existence of a country-wide road network. Much of the network may have been lost to the phenomenon of over-building. Britain's modern road system follows to some extent the Roman roads that preceded it. Those follow the Celtic roads that existed prior to Roman conquest and those possibly to even earlier transport systems. Little is known of the people who travelled the Neolithic roads. We are left to wonder whether deliveries to Stonehenge were the result of commercial initiative, cultural imperatives or religious pilgrimage.

No such central monument exists in the Alpine home of the Iceman. The remains of Neolithic Europe are scattered widely and found at random. The chance discovery of the Iceman gives us both a focal point for examination and a reality check for conclusions drawn from other sources.

The story of how the Iceman came to rest in an Alpine glacier begins with the thawing of another glacial mass more than six thousand years earlier. The last Ice Age came to an end around 9500 BC. Left in the wake of retreating glaciers were warm, damp, fertile lands. Over the next two thousand years agriculture gradually took root in the valleys of the great rivers of the Middle East; the Nile, the Tigris and the Euphrates.

Farming is often thought of as a sedentary occupation. It is actually a driver of expansion. The intensive nature of agriculture both requires and can support a large labor force per unit of land. Death from privation is less common. The resulting high survival rate leaves each succeeding generation larger than the last. As populations grow, so grows the need for new lands to cultivate. In Nineteenth Century AD America this led to westward migration to the Great Plains and beyond. In the prehistoric Middle East, the fertile plains of Anatolia were close at hand.

In the centuries following 7000 BC agriculture began to expand beyond Anatolia. During the Nineteenth and Twentieth Centuries AD scholars debated the nature of the expansion. The question was whether it involved an actual migration of farmers from Anatolia or simply represented an adoption of the concepts and procedures involved in farming by established hunter-gatherer populations in Europe.

Advances in DNA analysis in the early Twenty First Century AD established that a migration occurred. Further progress in analysis enabled scientists to extract and read ancient DNA. This provided a tool to track the movement of migrant farmers into and across Europe and to trace their interactions with other cultures.

The migration followed two distinct paths, sometimes referred to as the river route and the Riviera route. The river route was initially thought to begin with a crossing of the Bosporus around 6500 BC. In fact the Bosporus did not exist then. It, and the Black Sea, were created by a seismic event dated to 5500 BC. The river route followed the Danube from the Balkans into central Europe and then branched out along the Rhine around 5500 BC. The Riviera route took the migrants by boat to Crete around 6700 BC and to mainland Greece a century later. It moved along the Mediterranean coast of Europe through Greece, the Balkans, Italy, Southern France and Spain.

The migration followed an unusual leapfrog pattern. New settlements would be established a hundred or more miles ahead of the last. The space between would be filled in with new settlers during succeeding years. Eventually the river and Riviera routes reached the Atlantic coast. The Riviera route spread north and the river route spread north and south. Around 5000 BC, some fifteen hundred years after setting out from Anatolia, the two groups met and merged in the area around modern Paris. From there they spread farming culture into the rest of Europe.

The land they had moved into was virgin in the sense that it had never been farmed, but it was not empty. Hunter-gatherer groups had occupied the forests of Stone Age Europe for as much as forty thousand years. Scholars are still struggling to understand the interaction between the newcomers and the incumbent population. There was ample opportunity for a synergistic relationship. The migrants brought the wealth and security of agriculture. The incumbents possessed knowledge of the land: which edible plants grew well, which plants were medicinal and which were toxic. Hunting, fishing and tool making skills made them potentially valuable trading partners. On the other side of the coin was potential hostility between cultures, aggravated by the possibility of competition for the same lands. Whether one or the other prevailed seems to have varied by location.

DNA analysis established that the migrants and the incumbent population differed notably in physical appearance. The incumbent hunter-gatherers tended to be blue eyed, taller and more robust than the brown eyed migrants. Based on height, eye color and location of the Iceman's remains, he was a descendant of migrants arriving by the Riviera route.

DNA establishes that the migrants travelled in family groups rather than as largely male incursions. This was determined by the relative contribution of X and Y chromosomes in excavated burials. The culture is thought to have been patriarchal, at least in the sense that wealth, and presumably power, followed the male line. The relative wealth and security enjoyed by the farming culture may have attracted hunter-gatherer females to marriage or some other form of reproductive bonding, contributing to a merger of the two lineages. Analysis of isotopes in tooth enamel indicates a tendency for women to marry in from outside.

The migrant farmer culture absorbed rather than replaced the incumbent hunter gatherer population. Much of Europe's population soon contained a mix of DNA from both. Around 4500 BC, by which time agriculture was the established norm, there occurred what is termed a

Mesolithic (Middle Stone Age) resurgence in DNA. This does not imply any return to Middle Stone Age hunter-gatherer lifestyle. It simply reflects an increase in the percentage of hunter-gatherer DNA contribution in the population of the time.

There was a contemporary cultural shift evidenced by a change in burial practices. Previously individuals were buried in the ground. Beginning around 4500 BC one or two people were placed in chambers and those built over with large mounds. How or why this occurred is not known. It may be related to a trend to disproportionate distribution of wealth and resulting changes in social structure.

It was some time after this that the age of metals began, when humankind learned to smelt copper. How, when and where this began is not known. The process is far from simple. Copper ore (malachite) is only about ten percent metal. The metal has to be separated by melting it out of the native ore. The melting point of copper is almost 2000 degrees Fahrenheit. For a furnace to reach that temperature would require both charcoal fuel and some source of forced air, probably from a bellows.

Once the technology was mastered a large, dedicated labor force was required to extract useable amounts of the metal. Vast amounts of the ore would have to be dug out of the ground with primitive tools, often from considerable depth. Sizeable areas of forest would have to be felled and burned for charcoal. Furnaces would have to be manned and maintained. Mountains of tailings would have to be disposed of. The farming economy of the time must have advanced to the point where its surplus could support this activity.

Agricultural organization seems to have been village centered. A few sites excavated in Germany display a defensive structure. Centrally located was a large fortified village, surrounded at some distance by a ring of sparser settlements which in turn were surrounded by a ring of what the excavators referred to as frontier settlements. This bears some resemblance to the modern military philosophy of defense in depth. The philosophy dictates a sparsely garrisoned general outpost line to provide early warning of hostile approach. Behind that is a more densely manned combat outpost line to provide early interdiction and harassment of hostile advance. Finally there is a main line of resistance to stop hostile incursion and a reserve force to repel the invaders by counter-attack.

The comparison with recent tactical doctrine is tempting, but may not provide an accurate or complete picture. It is possible that the arrangement of settlements may have been dictated in whole or in part by economic efficiency or cultural preference. It is clear that the social climate of the time was marked by some level of violence. The fate of the Iceman stands as testimony to the dangers facing his contemporaries. Some level or organization may have been involved in his death, either through a general watch on his route or targeting based on specific knowledge of his itinerary. Supporting the notion of organized combat, there have been several random finds of burials of disarticulated human remains interred without any sign of the ceremonies normally found in burials of the period.

Normal burial patterns suggest the existence of social stratification. Excavation of inhumations involving both migrant farmers and incumbent hunter-gatherers tend to show more ritualistic treatment of migrant bodies, indicating a higher social status. This is not surprising. Agriculture is traditionally seasonal and labor intensive. It is reasonable that supervisory roles would be filled by knowledgeable migrants and that the incumbent population would be retained on an as-required basis to perform the labor of field preparation, planting and harvest. The situation likely persisted based on ancestry after the two populations began to merge. No evidence of meritocracy has been found.

Also missing is any evidence of central control. Political and social centers were localized. The urban centers growing in Egypt and Mesopotamia at the time of the Iceman are absent from the landscape of Europe. There was only ancestral culture to bind together the disparate settlements spread across the continent.

Cultural similarities and demand for diverse products would have encouraged commercial alliances to facilitate trade. Ambition and envy would have encouraged attempts at local conquest and levied requirements for defense. The same was true of Europe in the first half of the Twentieth Century AD. Alternately trade flourished and two world wars ravaged the continent. Subsequent events have healed the scars and rebuilt the physical and cultural landscape.

Europe just before 3000 BC was also on the verge of dramatic change. Once DNA researchers had sequenced The Iceman's genome, they set out to trace his lineage and find his modern descendants. There were no modern descendants. The Iceman's line had died out. The closest match was to the inhabitants of the isolated islands of Sardinia and Sicily, and to residents of the Southern Iberian Peninsula (Spain and Portugal). In the years following 3000 BC the culture that had produced the Iceman and populated Europe perished in the face of a new and deadlier migration.

DEATH RIDES A
PALE HORSE

W̲e touched briefly on the Yamnaya migration and its unique nature
during our consideration of the Hittites. While the Yamnaya were
not the likely source of the Hittites or their rise to imperial power in the
Eastern Mediterranean, they did have a profound impact on another,
far larger region. Before we examine that impact, it will be helpful to
understand who the Yamnaya were.

The name Yamnaya is derived from a Russian adjective that translates
roughly as *related to pits*. This refers to the culture's practice of burying their
dead in pits covered by mounds called kurgans. The Yamnaya culture arose
around 3300 BC in the Late Copper Age and faded away around 2600
BC in the Early Bronze Age. Both dates are necessarily approximations.
The tendency of following cultures to gradually absorb their predecessors
makes it difficult to establish precise chronological boundaries.

The Yamnaya culture originated in a region called the Pontic Steppe.
The area is generally bounded by the Southern Don, Ural and Dniester
Rivers. This places it at the eastern reach of modern Europe and the
western edge of modern Asia. Modern division of the Eurasian land mass
is arbitrary and would have meant nothing to the Yamnaya.

The Steppe is a vast grassland stretching about five thousand miles
from Eastern Europe to China. Settlement was widely scattered and
primarily limited to river valleys. Most of the region had too little rainfall

to support agriculture and too few watering sites to support large holdings of livestock. Scarcity and physical separation of the resources necessary for survival promoted the development of civilization in enclaves.

Enclaves do not imply isolation. The discovery of artifacts originating in the contemporary region of Uruk, far to the south in Mesopotamia, established the presence of long range commerce. That sort of interaction would not be likely to knit local groups together. The various enclaves of Steppe population had access to the same resources and had little, if anything, to trade with one another. Until the rise of the Yamnaya, the area was populated by a variety of independent local cultures. Cultural independence is inferred from the different styles of pottery used by each. This dissimilarity is generally taken to imply limited communication between cultures.

The culture is not ancestrally unique. It is classified among Western Steppe Herders, a group of cultures in the same region defined by similar ancestry. The common ancestry of the culturally dissimilar inhabitants of the East European and West Asian portion of the Steppe has been established by DNA analysis. Something more than half of the common ancestry was sourced from East Asian hunter-gatherers. This is an ancestry the Yamnaya would eventually carry westward into the rest of Europe and which later Europeans would carry farther westward across the Atlantic into America.

Parenthetically, this is the same ancestry from which the native North American population is derived. Before the end of the last Ice Age an eastward migration took East Asian hunter-gatherers across the Bering Strait land bridge into the Americas. This is not to suggest that Custer and Sitting Bull shared a common ancestor who lived thousands of years before they met at the Little Big Horn. It does, however, serve to underscore the vast differences in culture that can result from the need to adapt to differences in environment. And by extension to changes such as that produced by the Santorini eruption.

The remaining contribution to Western Steppe Herder DNA came chiefly from regions to the south, modern Armenia and Iran. The most likely route of influx is northward through the Caucasus, the region lying between the Black and Caspian Seas. The DNA contributors are generalized under the title Caucasian hunter-gatherers. This geographic reference is the source of the word Caucasian used in official modern ethnic differentiation. Ethnicity is one of the physical factors both determined by and used to classify DNA. Based on genetic make-up Western Steppe Herders tended to be tall for their time, dark haired and dark eyed, and lactose tolerant.

DNA can also provide a clue to the language spoken by Western Steppe Herders. Based on the known vocabulary of cultures established by DNA analysis to have descended from the Yamnaya, their language was some form of Indo-European. In the few areas of Europe not impacted by the Yamnaya migration non-Indo-European languages such as Basque prevailed. The fact that an Indo-European language travelled westward with the Yamnaya does not address the question of the ultimate source of the Indo-European language families.

The Yamnaya are associated with the early domestication of horses and the early adoption of wheeled vehicles. The earliest known wheeled cart was found in Ukraine, in a kurgan associated with the Yamnaya. Some sources have pictured the Yamnaya migration as an army sweeping across Europe in horse drawn chariots. This is pure fantasy. Their wagons were crude and suited mainly for cartage.

The Yamnaya did not originate the domestication of horses or the use of wheeled vehicles. These distinctions may belong to the Maykop Culture. Based on remains found to date, the Maykop appear to have been a sedentary population in the Caucasus. They had riverine access to the Sea of Azov. This in turn gave them access to the Black, Aegean and Mediterranean Seas. They were ideally positioned to trade with other Steppe Herders. The Maykop had few horses, but a bridle fitting has been found among their remains. Fragments of wooden wheels have also been excavated. Maykop petro glyphs have been discovered. So far they have defied translation.

In contrast, the Yamnaya were entirely nomadic. The mobility afforded by the horse and wagon allowed them to move constantly to find the best graze and most abundant water for their herds of sheep and cattle. This approach would have been attractive to the small local cultures that had been dependent on immediately available resources. In the years before

3000 BC the Yamnaya culture expanded across the Steppe, absorbing smaller, ancestrally similar cultures.

It has been theorized that the domestication of horses allowed the Yamnaya to manage larger herds and manage them more efficiently than they could have on foot. Eventually herd size outgrew the graze available in the semi-arid steppes and provided the impetus for migration. This is questionable. Nomadic Steppe herders still exist today in the far reaches of Mongolia, living as their ancestors did for thousands of years, without running water, electricity or roads. Their horses are used to extend their hunting range, not for herding. Traditionally the speed and aggressive nature of trained dogs offered the most efficient method of herd management.

As previously discussed, while the DNA of European humans traces back to the Yamnaya, the DNA of horses does not trace to a single source. This suggests that we should not form a picture of the Yamnaya sweeping across Europe on horseback like the later hordes of Genghis Khan. It is more likely that the techniques of domestication travelled westward with the Yamnaya rather than any great herds of domesticated horses. These techniques were then applied to local breeds encountered as the Yamnaya expanded westward.

It is unlikely that upgrades in transportation technology were enough to enable the Yamnaya migration into Europe. It is probable that the spread of Yamnaya culture across the Steppes brought some sort of political organization. This may or may not have followed the common pyramid model of a group of chiefdoms reporting up through a hierarchy of overlords, but organization of some type would have been required to enable large scale migration. Even a simple decision like which route to take would require either a command structure or some social mechanism for mutual agreement.

The Yamnaya were certainly aware of the fertile ground in lands surrounding them. They were also constrained in the routes available. The way to South Asia and the Indian subcontinent was blocked by the towering Hindu Kush. The way west provided two options. Moving south of the Black Sea would bring them into the Fertile Crescent and Mesopotamia. The land there was attractive but spoken for. Even as early as 3000 BC wresting it away from the incumbent population might require assaults on fortified cities and engagements with professional armies. The presence of trade goods from the Uruk civilization in cultures preceding the Yamnaya make it clear that commerce between Mesopotamia and the Steppe region was well established. The Yamnaya would have had a clear picture of what confronted them if they risked the south western route. The north western route promised more sparely settled land and less robust defenses.

The concept of sparsely settled is relative. Farming in Europe was not conducted on the intensive basis found in Mesopotamia, but the population density existing in the fertile areas of Europe around 3000 BC was still far greater than that found on the Steppes. For a smaller population to insinuate itself into the territory of a larger would have required, at least initially, some localized bullying. DNA analysis indicates the Yamnaya migration contained a higher than normal proportion of male to female participants. This suggests some level of military or quasi-military organization on the part of the Yamnaya.

The Yamnaya migration did not require outright conquest. The population of Europe at that time is estimated at no more than one percent of what it is today. Some areas settled by the earlier Anatolian farmer migration had been abandoned by the time the Yamnaya arrived. This does not imply an overall decline in the incumbent population. To cite a modern example, the American city of Detroit saw large scale abandonment of housing and small shops due to relocation of automobile manufacturing. At the same time the overall American population was increasing.

Abandonment was no more necessary than conquest. Vast tracts of European woodlands were available for newcomers to clear. There is some evidence of forest clearing at the time of the Yamnaya influx. Co-existence, hostile or otherwise, was certainly viable, and would have been necessary, if only temporarily, for the Yamnaya to absorb the agricultural knowledge required to make use of their new home. Even in primitive times, farming involved a great deal more than just putting seeds in the ground and hoping for the best. Planting and harvest cycles had to be observed, crops had to be processed and stored, land had to be fallowed to preserve fertility.

Something beyond conquest or abandonment must have occurred to enable the Yamnaya to replace the incumbent population in Europe.

The currently available archaeological and DNA evidence leaves no doubt as to the fact, the timing and the nature of the Yamnaya influx. At the time corresponding with the beginning of the Yamnaya migration a unique pottery style called corded ware appeared in Europe. Burial mounds similar to the kurgans found on the Steppes also began to show up in conjunction with this pottery style. DNA analysis of the remains from these burials established that the people interred had Steppe related ancestry. Buried with them were an assortment of the weapons that would have been required to either overcome or force a truce with the incumbent population which, as evidenced by the murder of the Iceman, was both skilled with weapons and willing to use them.

As we have discussed, some incumbent settlements also displayed experience in defensive organization. This implies some history of internecine conflict among the incumbent population. Pre-existing hostilities would have required the Yamnaya to deal with the incumbent population on a piecemeal basis.

Lactose intolerance suggests the incumbent population lived by farming supplemented by hunting and gathering. At most there would have been limited reliance on the milk of domesticated animals. The majority of the incumbents would have had no immunity to the diseases that can spread among populations engaged in the widespread herding of domesticated animals. Natural selection would have bred immunity among the new arrivals, allowing them to transmit the disease without suffering its consequences.

DNA testing has established the Yamnaya as plague carriers. The strain of plague was not the bubonic variety that later devastated Europe. Bubonic plague is a tick borne variation that was spread by rats travelling as scavengers on the trade routes of medieval times. The Yamnaya, in contrast, carried a strain of pneumonic plague that is spread by airborne contact. Sneezing and coughing are often cited, but ordinary respiration is more likely in the case of the Yamnaya migration. A large portion of the Yamnaya carrier population may not have displayed symptoms.

Plague, and pestilence in general, were well known and widely feared in the ancient world. Civilizations usually assigned responsibility to a god or goddess. Prayer and propitiation were the only available remedies. In Judeo-Christian scripture, where there was only one god, it ranks among the Four Horsemen of Apocalypse. The prophet Ezekiel mounts it on a pale horse and sends it forth along with war, famine and the beasts of the Earth to wreak havoc on humankind. Modern figures provide a relative order of magnitude. Estimates of deaths resulting from the four years of World War I range from fifteen to thirty million. Estimates from the two year Spanish flu epidemic that followed range from seventeen to one hundred million deaths.

Differences in the variety of plague pathogens and the environments into which they were introduced historically produced very different results. In Medieval Europe rapid trans-shipment of goods allowed near-simultaneous introduction of plague into densely populated urban centers where it could expand rapidly into an explosive epidemic that killed millions in a short space of time. The Yamnaya variety brought a far slower spread. Pathogens were introduced into scattered agricultural villages that had limited contact with one another. Transmission moved only as rapidly as the migration progressed. The Yamnaya replacement throughout Europe occurred over a span of centuries.

The details of transmission of the Yamnaya plague into Europe are not known. We can speculate based on the later introduction of European disease into the Americas. Initially the native and European populations co-existed in their own settlements. With the onset of greater interaction outbreaks occurred. Native settlements were devastated. Like the Yamnaya penetration into Europe, the situation evolved over centuries. It was around 2500 BC when the Yamnaya replacement took hold in Britain, the last westward bastion of the Anatolian agrarian-sourced culture. Even when it was complete, remote areas in Iberia and the Mediterranean islands retained their Anatolian farmer roots.

The Yamnaya migration involved more than physical movement and genetic replacement. The migration travelled in one general direction and was bounded by geography. Such was not the case with ideas. As an example, in the southern Iberian Peninsula, where the old agrarian culture persisted, pottery referred to as the bell beaker style came into common use. That style of pottery originated outside the reach of the Yamnaya migration, around 2700 BC. The style travelled northward and eastward, into the path of the migration. The Yamnaya adopted it and carried it westward with their migration. It has been found as far west as Britain.

During the five hundred years it took the Yamnaya migration to advance across Europe and replace the incumbent population, the migrants did more than absorb the agricultural knowledge necessary to prosper in their new land. They also fell heir to the metal resources, in particular the comparatively rare tin, which were used in the manufacture of bronze. This placed them in direct contact with the cultures at the forefront of the expanding Bronze Age. The domestication of horses and the use of wheeled conveyances brought a new efficiency to existing trade routes. More goods and ideas could move faster and farther.

Increased pace and volume would have required that the transshipment nodes of the expanded network grow larger. They would have been well short of urban in size, but still centers of administration and commerce. This was something neither the Yamnaya nor the incumbent population would have needed previously. Their world was evolving. The rise of the Minoan trading complex would have enhanced contact with distant corners of the world.

This leaves the question of how Europe changed between 2500 BC, when the migration was essentially complete, and the 1600 BC eruption of Santorini. On the available evidence, common DNA was not enough to unify Europe. Even today European unity is a fragile work in progress. The divisions are long standing. Julius Caesar opens his account of his extensive First Century BC European military campaigns with the famous phrase *All of Gaul is divided into three parts*. Earlier Greek writing mentions the Celts (Keltoi) as a European culture distinct from others. European languages suggest even earlier divergence. Germanic and romance languages, both from Indo-European roots, are notably different in structure.

The source(s) of European language variations is/are rooted in prehistoric times. In the absence of writing we are left to speculate. Some variation is probably related to the Yamnaya acquisition of agricultural skills from the people they eventually replaced. Acquisition of specialized knowledge would have required acquisition of the associated vocabulary.

Putting the knowledge to productive use would have required adopting some of the habits and characteristics of the incumbent population before it died out. Language might have been among those characteristics. The results would have been a hybrid of the original Yamnaya Indo-European and the existing languages specific to the areas they settled

The Yamnaya would also have fallen heir to the territorial imperatives of the incumbent population. Pre-existing competition for local resources may have split the Yamnaya, if indeed they were ever a tightly knit people. We do not know the details of their spread. We have only physical artifacts, Indo-European languages and the indelible stamp of DNA to attest to its occurrence.

The term migration as used in historical context is best understood as a synonym for expansion. The Yamnaya migrants did not abandon the Steppe. The disproportionately male structure of the migration indicates that family members remained in the Steppe. Commercial opportunities would have existed. Lines of communication would have been maintained. During the Middle Bronze Age ideas and technology flowed freely along Minoan trade routes. Once into Europe they could move without hindrance from the British Isles to the Steppe and impact cultures across the region. Bronze Age weapons and the concepts underlying professionalized war fighting emerged and spread during this period.

In the centuries following the murder of the Iceman the cultures of Europe and Western Asia had undergone profound change. Fragmented, mobile and technically capable, the region contained aggressive elements able to take decisive action when the time came to deal with the volcanic winter brought on by the Santorini eruption.

CHARIOTS OF THE GODS

The stratospheric winds that carried the sulfate aerosol veil from the Santorini eruption blew from west to east. Unlike lower level winds, they were neither hindered nor channeled by the terrain below. Prevailing atmospheric effects would have determined their precise path but would not have altered their overall direction. The graphics depicting the jet stream steering storms on the nightly television weathercast offer a visual representation of the situation. Volcanic winter would have spread in a band that circled the globe but did not extend north or south beyond certain latitudes.

Ice cores taken from Greenland have shown no residue traceable to the Santorini eruption. Dendrochronology has revealed signs of volcanic winter in the tree growth patterns of Northern Europe, so that latitude is probably the northern boundary. Since Egypt was seen as a refuge from the impact of Eastern Mediterranean volcanic winter, the latitude of its northern coast can reasonably be set as the southern boundary.

Eastern Europe and the Steppes lay in the path of the eastward spread of the aerosol veil. Crops and graze would have withered. Annual harvests would have diminished or failed entirely. Based on modern experience there would have been widespread loss of livestock. The population faced starvation. Those in the grip of volcanic winter had no idea how long it might last, or if it might be permanent. The only escape from the west to east band of sulfate aerosols was to move north or south.

The Indian Subcontinent offered one possible refuge. It had long been settled by the time of the Santorini eruption. The earliest urban settlements in the region known to modern scholars appeared in the Indus River Valley of what is now India and Pakistan, first at the city of Mohenjo Daro and later at Harappa. Our knowledge of these civilizations is based on archaeology begun between the First and Second World Wars. We do not currently have DNA from either civilization, so we cannot trace the populations to source. Both civilizations were literate, at least in the sense that they left a coherent set of written symbols behind. We have yet to decipher their language(s). Both cities had invested heavily in the construction of defensive walls, indicating that they expected and were prepared to ward off hostile encroachment. Their economies were based primarily on farming rather than herding. There is no evidence of the domestication of horses.

Additional walled settlements have been found in the Punjab and Sind regions, accommodating in total perhaps tens of thousands of residents and regional settlers. The presence in Mesopotamia and the Eastern Mediterranean of trade goods sourced from India suggest that a sophisticated network of settlement and commerce existed throughout the subcontinent well before the time of the Santorini eruption. The wealth of the region was certainly known to people in the north caught in the grip of volcanic winter.

People migrating to India from Eastern Europe and the Steppe region to escape the aftermath of the eruption faced daunting challenges. The first was the physical journey. Based upon choices of route by later travelers, the most likely was by way of the Khyber Pass, a tortuous defile through the Spin Ghar Mountains of Afghanistan. This is no easy trek, even with modern internal combustion engines. For any population to undertake the trip would require powerful motivation.

The Yamnaya had earlier elected to move westward from the Steppe around 3000 BC. Their successors would not have enjoyed that option in 1600 BC. Stratospheric winds can move in excess of two hundred miles an hour. They would have circled the globe and left Europe in the grip of the same volcanic winter that threatened the Steppe.

The second challenge facing refugees from the Steppe, as in the earlier migration, was overcoming or establishing co-existence with the incumbent population. The existence of fortified settlements made this a high risk venture that, again, would have required powerful motivation such as the aftermath of the Santorini eruption might have provided. Gradual infiltration was not possible. Conflict was almost certain. The outcomes favoring the migrants were conquest, enforced co-existence, absorption or replacement. Each of those would have left varying traces of DNA.

We do find evidence of northern DNA arriving in the population at the time of the eruption. The DNA is normally referred to as West Eurasian, and for convenience we will use that term. The timing is imprecise. The best available evidence supports a migration during the 2,000 years preceding the birth of Christ. While this does not specifically support a southward migration at the time of the Santorini eruption, it certainly allows the possibility. We will need to examine other evidence to further refine the timeline.

We have no decipherable contemporary writing from the Indian Subcontinent from that period, but we do have a work called the *Rig Veda*. It was committed to writing in Old Sanskrit some centuries later, but is thought to have been composed around 1500 BC, shortly after the eruption. Old Sanskrit is one of the Indo-European family of languages. Its shared vocabulary with and similarity in construction to European languages was one of the first clues that there might once have been a root Indo-European language.

The *Rig Veda* is the earliest of a set of Vedas, which are Hindu religious texts. These consist of books of hymns covering beliefs, customs, laws, prayers and, most importantly for our examination, history. Hymn 33 of Book 1 tells of Indra, the Hindu god of war, leading an Aryan army that destroyed the forts and seized the territory of the incumbent population, called the Daysus.

The timing is right for a hostile migration from the north driven by the consequences of the Santorini eruption, but a number of vague areas need to be resolved. The text does not give us a firm fix on whom the Aryans were or where they came from. Since the Daysus were defending fortified settlements it is reasonable to classify them as an incumbent population.

The *Rig Veda* does not tell us who the Daysus were nor does it offer any historical context in which to place the events described in the passages.

Also not addressed is the question of how long before the composition of the work the events took place. Since the text is religious in nature, and therefore to some extent faith-based, there is the additional question to what extent the reported events actually took place. We can reasonably infer that there is some element of truth. As in the case of Judeo-Christian scripture, the framers would have needed to build their work around a core of generally accepted fact to maintain credibility with their audience.

The timing can be refined to some extent by examining the fate of Harappa. Hymn 53 of Book 1 and Hymn 16 of Book 4 of the *Rig Veda* are specific about fortified areas being destroyed by Aryan armies. Harappa was abandoned, and appears to have been left fundamentally intact without noticeable battle damage. The abandonment occurred around 1800 BC, contemporaneous with a general shift in South Asian population from the Indus River valley to the Ganges. This would place the events of the *Rig Veda* at a later time.

Additional support for this constraint comes from the extensive mention of horses throughout the *Rig Veda*. Hymns 162 and 163 of Book 1 are devoted to the horse. Composition of the work must have occurred following the arrival in South Asia of domesticated horses, which post-dates the era of Harappa. Domesticated horses were a fixture in Europe and on the Steppe at the time.

A further indication of timing, as well as of the identity of the Aryans, is the mention of chariots in connection with horses. Hymn 12 of Book 2 specifically places horses and chariots under the control of Indra, the Hindu god of war. Warfare underwent substantial changes in the mid-second millennium BC. The compound curve bow laminated out of wood and animal horn provided a compact, powerful assault weapon capable of penetrating armor and engaging opposing forces at long range. Hymn 16 of Book 24 specifically connects the god of war with archery. The tactical utility of the laminated compound curve bow was greatly enhanced by modifications to the chariot, which had been in service for centuries mainly as a battle taxi for senior members of military command structures. The vehicle was adapted as an archery platform to provide the additional dimension of mobility to the power of the bow and expand its flexibility to permit massing of archery forces at critical points during battle. It was no accident that the Hindu god of war was prominently mentioned in connection with both chariots and archery.

The stability necessary to shoot accurately from a moving chariot was achieved in much the same way a smooth ride is provided in a modern automobile. The main carriage was spring mounted to absorb the impact from irregularities in terrain. Smoothness was maximized by the use of spoked rather than solid wheels to minimize the ratio of unsprung to sprung mass. Sophisticated woodworking techniques were needed to achieve the combination of flexibility and sturdiness to enable extended operations over difficult terrain at a weight light enough to avoid taxing the strength and stamina of the horses available at the time. The engineering and construction techniques underlying these modifications first appeared in the Eastern Mediterranean and expanded rapidly around the same time as the Santorini eruption.

While the use of chariot archery conferred great power, it also entailed substantial expense. Chariot horses required extensive training. Obtaining the vehicles in tactically viable quantities required either dedicated construction facilities or sufficient wealth to support commercial procurement. The additional requirements of repair and maintenance, crew training and the food, water and veterinary needs of a large stable of horses made chariot warfare a costly proposition. Archery also entailed cost. The time, material and expertise required to properly laminate a composite recurve bow limited their use to the elite.

Within a few centuries after the Santorini eruption battle tactics began to revert to more extensive use of infantry. Projectile delivery could be accomplished more cost effectively by foot archers with simpler wooden bows. Eventually war fighting progressed to the development of archery from individual horses. The timing of the evolution of war fighting places the events of the *Rig Veda* within a narrow window of time around the Santorini eruption. Factual elements within the *Rig Veda* indicate the presence of imported war fighting methods and machines.

The use of chariot archery by the armies of the *Rig Veda* is not sufficient by itself to establish the Aryans as originating from Europe or the Steppe. Chariots were widely used as archery platforms by most Middle Eastern military entities at the time. Hindu tradition, however, has provided a tool to aid in identification. Since the conquests cited in the *Rig Veda,* Indian society has functioned under a strict caste system. Discrimination based on the caste system was forbidden by law beginning in the Twentieth Century AD, but the system itself remains. Strict rules against intermarriage between castes have preserved the DNA of the individual castes across thousands of years.

The caste system (more properly systems), laid out in Vedas composed following the *Rig Veda,* is more complicated than we need to consider for our purposes. At the summary level is the Varna system that rank orders the population into primary categories. At the top are the Brahmins who are concerned with religious matters, next the warrior class, followed by a class of merchants, farmers and craftspeople, a class of laborers and finally an unclassified untouchable group.

By definition caste is a system of social exclusion and does not extend to commercial interaction. As a practical matter Brahmins are permitted to earn a living by engaging in the activities associated with the lower castes. Their primary duties concern the maintenance of purity, religious rites and sanctity. They are the logical heirs of the Aryans who were responsible for the original conquest.

Before we examine Brahmin DNA, a complex subject itself, we need to develop some appreciation of the complex process that resulted in the current population of the Indian Subcontinent. Initially there were indigenous hunter-gatherers. Around 7000 BC, a date established from the earliest settlements in the Indus valley, farmers from Iran began to infiltrate, bringing their cereal crops. It took some time to fully adapt these to the monsoon climate prevailing in much of the subcontinent. Around 5000 BC rice farming technology arrived, probably from an origin in China. Subsequent invaders from Alexander the Great to the Mughals of Afghanistan to some extent the British have left their mark. This has made for a wide range of physical features and spoken languages.

Those factors suggest we should expect more of a stew than a lineage when we examine DNA from the Indian Subcontinent. In fact, there is no evidence of genetic purity in any major Indian population group. Conclusions will need to be drawn based on percentage of contribution of each type to Brahmin DNA. This makes the timing of arrival of each element as well as the content of DNA critical in sorting out the question of Brahmin origins.

Analysis of ancient DNA from the country of India proper is further complicated by modern political sensitivities. Conclusions regarding ancient DNA can bear directly on the lineage claims of modern groups. Since raw data is open to multiple interpretations, there is legitimate concern that published findings may be unintentionally inflammatory. Accordingly, the Indian government restricts DNA testing so that no material is sent out of the country for examinations that can be performed at facilities in the country. Even with this restriction, we are still able to draw valid conclusions from the available information.

Examination of DNA from the Brahmin caste requires sampling from a number of subdivisions of the caste. As a side note, the overall complexity of the caste system makes it seem unlikely that the system was invented on the spur of the moment following the Aryan conquests on the Indian Subcontinent. It may be an extension of a pre-existing system of social stack-ranking of the conquering society to accommodate and absorb the existing stratification of the conquered population. This possibility is reflected in the results of Brahmin DNA studies. Across both geography and sub-castes Brahmins have a higher percentage of West Eurasian DNA than other castes in physical and economic proximity to them.

The picture is very different from that which emerged following the Yamnaya migration into Europe. The European migration resulted in wholesale population replacement. In India the migrants eventually merged with the incumbent population. Two factors may have driven this trend. First, the Indian subcontinent had a robust maritime trade in place. To gather goods on the coast for shipment required the existence of a sophisticated commercial network to move them from inland points of production. It would have been counter-productive to subject such a network to the sort of destructive conquest described in the *Rig Veda*. Even more compelling was the numerical discrepancy between the migrants and the incumbent population. There were too many incumbents to conquer. Once the migrants had reduced the incumbents' fortified centers of resistance, the practical approach was accommodation and infiltration.

The texts composed and maintained by the Brahmin caste are in Old Sanskrit, which is rooted in Indo-European. Lower castes tend to have DNA components associated with Southern India. The language used in the south is Dravidian, which is not Indo-European in origin. The Brahmins who migrated into the south and eventually came to speak Dravidian also tend to have DNA concentrations closer to those of Northern India. This supports the other indications of a hostile migration from West Eurasia, resulting in conquest in the north of the subcontinent followed by gradual infiltration of the south.

The population of modern India is the accumulated result of a stream of events. The original hunter-gatherer population was absorbed by an agricultural migration from Iran. Further migration from the orient added to the mix. Over the following centuries there developed a wide range of crafts and a complex commercial network. The Santorini eruption brought a further migration, this time from West Eurasia a little after 1600 BC, first into the north as the conquerors described in the *Rig Veda,* and then filtering southward to mix with the incumbent population.

Unfortunately the notion of a historical conquest of India by a European race, which predated the DNA evidence by many decades, became highly politicized and understandably unpopular in the Twentieth Century AD. With the rise of the National Socialist Party in Germany, the term Aryan became associated with the myth of a master race destined to conquer inferior races until it ruled the world. The swastika, the traditional Hindu symbol of good luck, was co-opted as the emblem of the Nazi movement. So deeply ingrained is the association with Nazism that even today American and European travelers are surprised to see the swastika prominently displayed in Asia. The idea of migration from Eastern Europe and the Steppe region resulting in the conquest of the Indian Subcontinent fell out of favor for reasons having nothing to do with historical or scientific evidence.

The Aryan conquest of India and the spread of Hindu religion are historical facts, as evidenced by the West Eurasian DNA left by the Aryans and the Indo-European roots of the Sanskrit language. Some scholars have gone as far as to draw parallels between the pantheon of Hindu gods and those of Greece and Scandinavia, suggesting roots in the same ancient source. Modern Europeans might be disturbed by the idea that the alien gods of the Hindu pantheon originated with their own ancestors. Modern Indians might be disturbed by the idea that their gods rode in on the chariots of foreigners. We are all connected in some way by the events of the distant past.

The timing of the conquest is set by DNA analysis during the two thousand years preceding the birth of Christ. It can be further bracketed by the end of Harappan civilization around 1800 BC, which predated the conquest, and the composition of the *Rig Veda* around 1500 BC, which described it. Within this time frame there was only one event that could have driven sizeable numbers of people out of West Eurasia and south across the forbidding mountains of Afghanistan. That is the volcanic winter associated with the Santorini eruption. Those in its grip would have had no knowledge that it would ever end. All they would have known was that it was not survivable for any length of time. Their only hope lay in migration.

The Santorini eruption did not create modern India. It was one step in a process that went on for thousands of years. Not all of the pieces of the puzzle of how modern India came to be are in place. Early migrations from Iran and East Asia are understood only in general terms. Two other key items missing are the DNA and language(s) of the Indus Valley civilizations of Mohenjo Daro and Harrapa. This does not minimize the impact of the Santorini eruption in molding the nation as it exists today. It was the Aryan refugees from volcanic winter who brought Hindu religion and a social organization that still prevails through much of the country.

The eastward movement of Santorini's volcanic winter did not stop with the Steppe. The global reach of the stratospheric winds carried the sulfate aerosol veil over the vast reaches of China. There the population did not have the luxury of an untainted destination to which to migrate.

DRAGON BONES

D NA evidence provides considerable insight into the impact of the Santorini eruption on the culture of the Indian Subcontinent. When we trek eastward to China, the trail of ancient DNA goes cold. The current Chinese government maintains strict controls over the export of the human skeletal material needed for DNA analysis. Local national scientists have released little DNA information from their own studies. The extent of their studies is not known with certainty outside China. As a result, little in the way of the evidence needed to construct a cohesive narrative of descent is available for our examination.

Based upon the limited information that has come into general circulation, analysts have hypothesized the existence of two ghost populations, which are the main ancestral groups of modern Chinese. A ghost population is one which DNA analysis indicates should exist to create a trail of descent from known earlier populations to known later populations, but for which no physical findings exist that can be used to develop a genome. The Yamnaya first existed in the DNA literature as a ghost population. It was some time before their genome was developed and their impact on European ancestry was established.

The two ghost populations in China still awaiting publication of a genome are associated with the country's two great rivers, the Yellow and the Yangtze. Their basins are the twin cradles of Chinese civilization.

The Yellow (Huang He) River makes its way some 3,400 miles through the north of the country and empties into the Bohai Sea south of modern Beijing. It is the sixth largest river system in the world, with a drainage area of more than 300,000 square miles. The ghost population of the area is associated with early agriculture involving the cultivation of millet and other grains.

The behavior of the Yellow River meant that cultivation of grains in Northern China differed from that practiced in Egypt and Mesopotamia. In Egypt the Nile flooded annually and replenished soil nutrients leeched out by the previous year's intensive farming. All that was needed to resume cultivation in the next season was a re-survey of farm boundaries. In Mesopotamia the Tigris and Euphrates were tamed by a series of dykes and irrigation canals. Flooding of the Yellow River in China devastated rather than deposited. It was too violent to be controlled by early Neolithic water management techniques. Floods on the Yellow River are the only natural disasters in recorded history to have taken more than a million lives. In places the river's fury presents a challenge even for modern engineering.

No successful management of the Yellow River was developed until the end of the Neolithic Period. Stone Age agriculture was conducted on a slash and burn basis. Land bordering the flood plain was cleared and then farmed until it was so devoid of nutrients that it could no longer produce viable crops. The farmers abandoned their village and moved on to clear and plant virgin soil. When that failed some years later and a period of fallow had replenished the soil nutrients on their original land they could return and rebuild on the foundations of the old village.

The village appears to have been the basic social and economic unit of a civilization tied together by common culture and commerce. This civilization predates writing. We are left to craft a picture of a primitive agricultural society based on analysis of archaeological findings and inferences drawn from the results.

The Yangtze is the greater of China's two major rivers. It winds for some 3,900 miles to empty into the East China Sea at Shanghai. It is the third longest river system in the world. Its drainage basin covers one fifth of the land area of China. The modern Three Gorges Dam project on the Yangtze is the largest hydroelectric power plant in the world. From early times the river has been navigable up to a thousand miles inland.

Cultivation of rice along the Yangtze River speaks volumes about the sophistication of the society practicing this form of agriculture. The process is complex. First, protected seed beds are planted. When the resulting sprouts are about eight inches high, fields need to be plowed, organic fertilizer applied and then flooded to a depth of eight inches. The sprouts are then transplanted laboriously by hand into the flooded fields, and the fields kept flooded throughout the growing season. When the rice is mature, the fields are drained and the rice harvested. The technology involved highly developed water management techniques that could flood fields to a prearranged depth without sluicing away nutrient rich soil.

In the Stone Age, before the advent of machines, this would have called for high orders of labor skill and management. Stable social organization was required for this to be carried out on a culture-wide scale. Again, the activity predates writing so we are reliant on relics, residue and inference to piece together the story.

The origin of agriculture in China can be traced back as far as 7000 BC, approximately contemporaneous with the development of cultivation in Anatolia. Current thinking favors independent development in the two areas, although knowledge of the origin of agriculture is still rudimentary. The first crops began as natural plants familiar to hunter-gatherer populations. It took centuries for these to mutate into recognizable products of agricultural effort.

Currently available analytical techniques do not allow us to pinpoint either the origin or origins of agriculture, either in location or time. Radiocarbon dating does allow archaeologists to establish the time frame of ancient settlements. The relics and refuse determine what crops were grown and how primitive the methods of cultivation were. Unlike later urban centers, whose locations can often be seen in high resolution satellite photographs, settlements are too small and their remains too deeply buried to be discerned. Agricultural settlements earlier than those currently known may be awaiting discovery.

Parallel with cultivation was the need to defend crops from predatory neighbors. In the case of the Yellow River civilization the primary threat originated on the North China plain. This was an area of sparse rainfall ill-suited to agriculture. Like the Steppe, it was an area of grassland adaptable to herding.

It is theorized that a military component of society arose from the need for protection and conferred power on those who controlled it. Stronger groups absorbed the weaker. From this grew a succession of Neolithic cultures. A general timeline of major known cultures places the Yangshao between 5000 and 3000 BC, the Liangzhu between 3300 and 2200 BC and the Longshan between 3000 and 2000 BC. The land area of China is vast and archaeologists still encounter cultures not previously known to exist.

The known cultures are not thoroughly understood. An example is the ability of Stone Age people to work the extremely hard mineral jade, specifically the version called nephrite, a silicate of calcium or magnesium. The mineral is too hard to be cut or flaked with other materials. It can only be worked by drilling or grinding. In modern times this involves laser technology and ultra high speed drills. How Neolithic Chinese cultures accomplished this is not known. Nor is it known by what trade routes the mineral was moved from the limited sources of supply in the Yangtze basin, Liaoning Province and Inner Mongolia.

There are indications that writing had reached an embryonic stage during the late Neolithic period. Something more than a hundred repeated symbols have been catalogued. Although Chinese writing has remained pictorial rather than following the western progression through syllabic to alphabetic, the Stone Age symbols are archaic. Given the limited number available, no translation is possible. Writing comprehensible by modern scholars was not practiced until after the arrival of metal technology.

The Bronze Age arrived in China around 2000 BC. Whether the original technology was imported or locally developed remains an open question. Adoption of the new technology called for a higher order of social and commercial organization. By this time the structure of Chinese civilization is generally expressed as dynasties rather than cultures. Wealth and power were vested in single families.

This organizational model persisted for thousands of years. It appears to have survived the Communist takeover of the country in the Twentieth Century AD. Extensive journalistic investigation has uncovered a maze of offshore companies and banking relationships which the current leaders of China have constructed to bypass the legal and philosophical constraints of communism to accumulate individual wealth and transfer it to their heirs.

Chinese history holds that a succession of five emperors came to power in the waning days of the Longshan culture. Whether their reputed accomplishments can be attributed to five individuals or simply represent the accumulated achievements of the Neolithic period remains a matter of speculation. Prior to their rise leaders were selected by the acclaim of the cultures involved. At the end of the reign of the five emperors the dynastic succession of leadership was put in place. The transfer of power became a matter of birth right. Prominent at the time of the arrival of bronze was the Xia Dynasty, holding sway in the area of the Yellow River. The Xia were the first of the Chinese dynasties. They set the pattern for thousands of years to follow.

Our knowledge of the late Neolithic period and the Xia Dynasty comes from three written sources. None of these are contemporary with the Xia Dynasty. The earliest is the *Book of Documents.* Included are speeches from the Zhou Dynasty, which seized power from the Shang Dynasty, supposedly at the mandate of heaven. The Shang had used a similar rationale for the seizure of power from the Xia Dynasty. The second source is Sima Qian, who was appointed historian of the Han court around 107 BC. He collected all the old writings that had survived a nationwide book burning a century earlier and compiled a 130 chapter history of China. His history mentions the use of bronze during the Xia dynasty. Archaeological exploration of Xia sites has since confirmed this. The *Bamboo Chronicles,* which we will examine in detail later, report the Xia in a succession of Dynasties.

In 1996 AD the current Chinese government commissioned a Xia-Shang-Zhou chronology project. The finding was that the Xia Dynasty ruled from 2070 BC until 1600 BC. The end date of 1600 BC, which is the date most critical to our examination, was established by radiocarbon dating of an urban foundation at Yanshi.

Archaeological finds from the Xia Dynasty include an imperial sized palace complex dated to about 1700 BC. This would have represented the top of the Xia hierarchy. The lowest level socio-political unit of the Xia kingdom was the walled town. Several such towns made up a vassal state. Each state was ruled by a clan or tribal leader who owed allegiance to the king. This political structure was well suited to changes that brought both reform and uniformity to agriculture. The early Neolithic slash and burn style of farming an area out and then moving on had been replaced by a system in which some land in each community was allowed to lie fallow and replenish its nutrients. This removed the need for regular relocation and brought local stability.

Military activity during the Xia Dynasty was the exclusive province of the nobility. A standing professional army would have been necessary to repel hostile incursion, secure commerce against banditry and suppress internal dissent. The composition, strength and disposition of the Xia army are not known with certainty. Some later histories suggest considerable forces were under the control of clan leaders subordinate to the Dynasty. Ambition led to open hostility among the clan leaders. Fighting spiraled out of control and led to a state of anarchy. This scenario is questionable. There is general agreement that the Shang takeover required several years of hard fighting. This indicates a determined and centrally controlled resistance by the Xia.

The true nature of the Xia dynasty is obscured by contradictions. Some of the surviving history and legend portrays the Xia rule as descending into corruption and decadence that was brought to an end by the righteous rise of the succeeding Shang dynasty. How much of this is true and how much is propaganda is not clear. Many Chinese today look on the Xia dynasty as a golden age. Tradition cites the Huaxia as ancestors of the Han Chinese. Archaeological work has established the Xia Dynasty as contemporaneous with the Bronze Age Erlitou culture. Based on excavation of remains of their infrastructure, Erlitou represented a transitional society between village centered Neolithic civilization and the urbanized Shang Dynasty.

The Xia did develop a pictorial style of writing, but there is no contemporary historical narrative from either the Xia or succeeding Shang dynasty. The decipherable writing that does exist comes to us in the form of what are called Dragon Bones, sometimes westernized under the name Oracle Bones. Most of these are not actual bones, but tortoise shells, although some bones from oxen were used. These were prepared by the priests of the Shang Dynasty, who would write a question to the heavens on the bones and then heat them until they cracked. The cracks were then interpreted and the answers written on the bones. Tens of thousands of these inscriptions have been recovered.

Mentioned on a few of the Dragon Bones that have survived from the Shang Dynasty is the enemy province of Qi. Later written history identifies the province of Qi as the location to which the surviving leadership of the Xia Dynasty were exiled after the Shang took power. Mention of Qi in contemporary Shang writing provides a factual anchor for later histories and helps establish these histories as more than simply myth.

The oldest written history is found today in a text called the *Bamboo Chronicles*. Its survival was a fortuitous accident. The original was buried with a Chinese emperor and not found for centuries. As a result it escaped the massive book burning that took place in the interim. As with many ancient texts, we have only an incomplete copy, or in this case two copies. One is called the current copy, and is an abridged version of the original. The textual content of this copy is disputed. The other is called the ancient copy, and has been pieced together to the extent possible based on quotations and other historical material.

The Xia Dynasty ended in 1600 BC, with the rise of the Shang Dynasty, contemporaneous with the Santorini eruption. Such evidence as we have suggests this was not a coincidence. The *Bamboo Chronicles* mention a phenomenon in which three suns were observed. This is consistent with the refraction of light by the stratospheric sulfate aerosol veil during a volcanic winter. Other reports detail catastrophic failures of the Yangtze River Delta rice crop. By Chinese tradition the heavens sent natural calamities to serve notice that they were removing the incumbent dynasty's mandate to rule. It is intriguing to wonder whether this tradition might have originated with the simultaneous coming of Santorini's volcanic winter and the end of China's first dynasty.

Chinese history holds that the rise of the Shang Dynasty was made possible by a rising of peasants determined to unseat their rulers. Arming peasants would have gone against centuries of tradition in which only the nobility and their professional retainers were armed or participated in combat. In addition, it would have required that a large peasant group abandon their livelihood and put their lives at risk. In the absence of a widespread and powerful motivating force such as the volcanic winter following the Santorini eruption this seems highly unlikely.

Shang propaganda to the effect that the end of the Xia Dynasty was brought about by corruption and decadence does not explain large scale peasant revolt. The peasants were subordinate to a regime that had kept them at a successful subsistence level for more than four centuries. They had little motivation to trade one set of overlords for another. A far more likely scenario is that volcanic winter destroyed the peasants' agricultural livelihood. Under such conditions it could be argued that the heavens no longer favored the Xia Dynasty. Their priests had failed to predict the catastrophe and their entreaties failed to reverse it. The peasants took up arms under the Shang banner to answer the mandate of heaven and bring an end to the Xia Dynasty and the natural calamity it had spawned.

The natural passing of volcanic winter would have worked in the Shang Dynasty's favor. The end of the calamity following their rise to power would have bolstered the Shang claim that they enjoyed the favor of the heavens. More importantly, it gave peasants an opportunity to return to peaceful and productive agriculture. Arming peasants to overthrow the government set a dangerous precedent. With the peasant army that brought them to power disarmed and disbanded, the Shang faced to no real internal threat. They were free to use their professional military for conquest.

The militaristic Shang Dynasty spread its influence widely throughout the Yellow River basin and beyond. While the Xia Dynasty was wealthy and powerful, they functioned in a relatively limited geographic area. The Shang Dynasty grew to control many times the land area held by the Xia. The Shang were the first urban culture in what had been a predominantly rural society. The growth of cities concentrated crafts and commerce, and facilitated the growth of both. This growth broadened the economic base, which in turn led to a more stable society. The consolidation of China as we know it today was still more than a thousand years in the future, but the aftermath of the Santorini eruption set in place the pillars upon which it was built.

Any contemporary records the Shang left behind chronicling their initial takeover were likely lost when the succeeding Zhou Dynasty seized power and substituted their own version of history. Any self-aggrandizing inscriptions that might have been buried with the rulers vanished when the tombs of the Shang Emperors were plundered in later years. The only relatively intact tomb found in the Shang capitol of Amyang was that of Fu (noble woman) Hao, an imperial wife and female general who lived some three hundred years after the rise of the Shang. No written records of any historical consequence were found, only a few dragon bones offering random glimpses into the events of her life.

The abrupt end of the Xia Dynasty and the violent rise of the Shang in their place contemporaneous with the Santorini eruption cannot be dismissed as coincidence. There were certainly economic and cultural factors in play, but those had existed for long periods of time without bringing about violent overthrow of the existing order. Something had to happen to tip the existing balance and trigger change. The available clues point to the resulting volcanic winter as the primary motivating force.

From China the stratospheric winds spread Santorini's sulfate aerosol veil across the Pacific, bringing volcanic winter to the Americas. A distant and wild land, long disconnected from the Eurasian land mass and its civilizations, America was home to cultures that had adapted far differently from those of the East Asians, from whom their people descended.

WINTER IN THE
NEW WORLD

Our knowledge of the drama of human migration into the Americas is in the process of being re-scripted. Long cherished scenarios are collapsing under the weight of emerging evidence, often being replaced by more questions than answers. We will take a brief look at the current state of knowledge to build a foundation for our examination of the impact of Santorini's volcanic winter.

Native American is the term normally applied to the descendants of migrants who occupied the two continents prior to the European arrival. The term is a contradiction. It is not possible to be native and a migrant at the same time. It is valid, however, to lump the many tribes and nations involved into a single group. According to the best available information, they descended from the same source population. Since the term Native American has both official standing and wide acceptance, we will use it with the caveat that it is not intended as an accurate descriptor, but rather as a convenient label.

The peopling of the Americas has been the subject of sometimes acrimonious scholarly debate for more than a century. Current thinking has the process beginning in earnest around 22000 BC. This was the height of the most recent Ice Age. Massive glaciers covered large parts of the Earth. The water to create these glaciers had to come from somewhere, and the result was a drastic reduction in sea level. The distance from

Australia to Asia was greatly reduced, and what we now know as the Bering Strait between Russia and Alaska was dry land. This opened new routes of overland migration for Old Stone Age populations.

Migration into America proper was constrained by the massive glaciers that covered the northern reaches of the continent, as far south as Minnesota. The only viable route was a narrow coastal corridor stretching from Alaska southward along the shores of the Pacific. The area was rich in kelp, fish and nutrient plants. It would have been able to support migrants making the slow trek along this path looking for a more welcoming environment. An immigrant site dated to around 22000 BC has been found on the Alaska coast. Many others probably lie submerged on the continental shelf, inundated when the glaciers melted and sea levels rose. DNA sampling from a later site in Alaska matches DNA taken from remains at a site in Montana, establishing that the Alaska migrants were the source population for Native Americans as a whole.

The earliest identified culture in North America was the Clovis People, named for the town in New Mexico near where their residue was first located. They came on the scene around 12400 BC, as the area was gradually warming, and perished abruptly around 10800 BC when a sudden shift to lowering temperatures known as the Younger Dryas period took hold. The sudden climate change brought a phenomenon known as the Pleistocene Extinction. North American mega-fauna including mammoths, mastodons, saber tooth tigers, horses and camels were victims of the extinction. The Clovis culture had subsisted by hunting mega-fauna, and died out with their prey.

The Younger Dryas period is worth a brief excursion. It provides an example of the impact of a powerful natural force. A dark mantle of geologic debris deposited at the time indicates the period was the result of a hyper-velocity cosmic impact. A comet was drawn into an orbit that intersected that of Earth. Gravitational forces broke up the rocky interior of the comet. A number of the pieces struck the Earth at immense speed. We had a first-hand look at the power of the impact of comets in 1994 AD when fragments of Shoemaker-Levy ripped into the Planet Jupiter with explosive fury.

The rain of projectiles that struck not only North America but also the rest of the Earth around 10800 BC lasted twenty one years. This has been verified by higher than normal deposits of platinum in Greenland ice cores dated to around 10800 BC, and further validated by tests on the Younger Dryas mantle found at widely spread locations around the world. As a point of interest, the orbit of the comet still intersects that of Earth annually. Fragments are visible as a meteor shower.

To give a sense of the power of the twenty one years of impacts, an inbound extraterrestrial object exploded in an airburst over Tunguska in Siberia in recorded history (1908 AD) releasing up to fifteen megatons (millions of tons of TNT) of energy. This is the equivalent power of a hydrogen bomb. Forests were leveled for more than 750 square miles. The night sky lit up as far away as Britain. Only the remoteness of the impact saved humankind from a major catastrophe. This was a single event.

The twenty one years of impacts at the onset of the Younger Dryas period had a more complex and devastating outcome. They set expansive wildfires and did massive damage to the Canadian ice cap. Smoke from the wildfires obscured the sun for months at a time, creating the equivalent of today's concept of nuclear winter. The damage to the ice cap sent masses of cold water into the Atlantic Ocean, bringing sea levels up by as much as twelve feet and reversing the course of the Gulf Stream, which warms the Atlantic coast of North America. The cold spell triggered by the impacts lasted some 1,200 years. It was 9600 BC when America recovered from the renewed chill.

The inhabitants of America in the aftermath of Younger Dryas were hunter-gatherers subsisting on smaller game and surviving vegetation. We have the skeleton of one, the so-called Kennewick Man, from about 7400 BC. Orthopedic trauma attests to a robust outdoor life. DNA establishes that his closest living relatives are aborigines from the Japanese Islands, helping to validate that the source population of America began its trek in East Asia.

DNA analysis raises the possibility of multiple East Asian sources. An ancient population of the Amazon basin displays not only East Asian hunter-gatherer DNA, but also a contribution from Australia. This by itself is not surprising. During the Ice Age, Asia was far more accessible from Australia and interbreeding was likely. The Australian contribution was found in South America, but nowhere in North America. A north to south migration from a single source should have left traces all along its route. It is probable that the migrants carrying the Australian DNA signature simply failed to establish themselves in North America in numbers sufficient to leave traces today.

The Australian DNA signature is found in and around the Amazon River basin. The journals of early Spanish explorers tell of a large and sophisticated population in this region. That name Amazon comes from a Spanish sighting of female archers, leading to a comparison with the Amazons of classical literature. The land became known as Amazonia. Outbreaks of disease such as smallpox and influenza so devastated the population in later years that the Spanish journals were for a time discredited. No one believed the Amazon rain forest could support a large population.

The soils of rain forests are notoriously nutrient poor. The current year's growth of the forests is nourished by the decay of the previous year's detritus. The settlers of the Amazon basin were able to develop a special soil, usually referred to as dark earth that maintained fertility for long periods of time. Even now it is not well understood how this happens. The secret is believed to be in the microbial content of the soil.

The ecological makeup of areas chosen for settlement certainly had more to do with the survival of migrants than their DNA. While the study of ancient DNA has upset many of last century's theories and set scholars on the right track in many areas, it doesn't provide all the answers. In some cases it has drawn our attention to situations we had never before considered. The staple line for situation comedy actresses, *if you were the last man on earth, I'd consider dating outside my species,* turns out to be the source of some of our DNA. Ancient humans did interbreed with non-human species.

Neanderthals are the best known non-human species to produce offspring with humans. Anywhere from one to four percent of modern non-African DNA is sourced from Neanderthals, with the average running just over two percent. A second non-human group, called Denisovans, also contributed an average of around two percent to non-African DNA. Interbreeding did not stop there. A recently analyzed bone from a Siberian cave turns out to be from the offspring of a Denisovan father and a Neanderthal mother.

Interestingly, while the physical remains of Denisovans were discovered in Siberia, DNA analysis suggests they may have originated and flourished in Australia. Ancient DNA from Australia shows as much as a six percent Denisovan contribution. Further confusing the situation in the Amazon basin, settlers there with Australian DNA show very low concentrations of Denisovan DNA.

The clues and confusion offered by DNA analysis have come to us very recently, some as little as two years prior to this writing. The accelerating pace of ongoing research suggests more of both await us in the near future. For now we will have to be content to use them as an arrow pointing to places we can look to get an idea of where civilization stood in the Americas at the time of the Santorini eruption.

Ancient humankind found its greatest prosperity in the basins of the world's great river systems. The survival of Australian DNA in the Amazon basin when it did not survive anywhere else that we currently know of suggests the same is true in the rest of the Americas. The Amazon is too far south to have been impacted by the volcanic winter that followed the Santorini eruption. Tree ring data from California bristlecone pine provides an approximation of the impact zone. The major river system corresponding to that latitude is the Mississippi, and its large tributaries, the Ohio and the Missouri.

Unfortunately the influx of later European settlers was also drawn to the fertile river basins of North America. Farming and subsequent development resulted in wholesale destruction of Native American settlements and monumental sites. This was true not only in the river basins, but across the entire country. Remaining sites are found at random in unlikely places. One is on the grounds of Louisiana State University. Another on a golf course in Newark.

A common denominator in the Mississippi and tributary basins is the construction of mounds. This tradition was in place five thousand years ago and persisted until at least 800 AD. The purpose(s) of the mounds is (are) not known. Social status, religious ceremony and astronomical alignment have all been suggested. Unlike the Near East, where wood was rare and stone the construction material of choice, settlers in much of America made use of the perishable wood in plentiful forests. Little has survived.

The mounds appear to have nothing in common with the shelters of the nomadic plains people, the pueblos of the southwest or the fishing villages of the northwest. This implies variation in the economic and cultural underpinnings of the societies involved. We have only the remains of their sites to tell their story.

When archaeologists excavate an ancient site, they look for clues that will help them classify the site and the people associated with it. The classifications are numerous. One is the purpose of the site; whether it was intended for habitation, ritual purposes, storage or some combination. Another is the capability of the builders; specifically whether they were members of a Stone Age civilization or made use of metal tools. Also whether the basis of their economy was hunting and gathering, or whether they had progressed to agriculture. Economic level is also important. Subsistence level sites are those in which most or all of the activities carried out were concerned with the provision of food, clothing and shelter for the immediate inhabitants. Higher level sites are those where most of the activities were concerned with administration or commerce. Most important for our examination of the impact of the volcanic winter associated with the Santorini eruption is the time frame during which the site was active.

Although Native North Americans left no written record of their history, many of their customs persisted into the historical period following the arrival of European immigrants. Knowledge of the purpose of various sites was preserved as a result of contact with literate European newcomers. An example is the Medicine Wheel site in the Big Horn Mountains of Wyoming. This is a ritual site where the chosen were allowed to go to fast and receive visions. The occurrence of visions is probably not fiction. The site is at an altitude of some nine thousand five hundred feet above sea level. The air is thinner at that height, and mild oxygen deprivation in connection with fasting could induce hallucinations. Other ritual sites clearly serve mortuary purposes, which conforms to modern Native American concern with culturally appropriate burial of their dead.

For some ritual sites, we have no clear understanding. The best known of these is Serpent Mound, a quarter-mile long man-made earthwork in Ohio thought to represent a giant serpent. Advancing theories about the monument has long been a favorite pastime of scholars. Answers to the questions of why it was built and what it was used for remain as elusive now as they were the day it was discovered. It stands as a reminder that our body of questions about American prehistory is far larger than our body of knowledge.

The purpose(s) of habitation and storage sites is often clear from excavated remains. Garbage dumps and dried human feces can provide detailed information on diet, clothing, tools and other facets of daily life. This in turn allows us to categorize the occupants according to whether they were hunter gatherers or farmers, and whether they used stone tools or had adopted metal. The excavated residue may contain carbon-based items that allow us to determine the time frame in which the site was in use.

The character of sites actively occupied at the time of the Santorini eruption varies according to geographic location. The fishing sites of the Pacific Northwest, for example, differ greatly in from sites on the Lower Mississippi, where fishing was also practiced. Hunting practices in the wooded northeast differ from those on the open prairie. In spite of unique character, all of the known occupation sites from this period indicate occupation by Stone Age hunter gatherers.

Metal was not unknown at the time. Copper was readily available to natives in the area of Lake Superior. The lake is at the south end of a large land formation called the Canadian Shield. Glaciers had scrubbed this area down to bedrock and exposed deposits of copper, pieces of which could be broken loose by heating and shock cooling. The metal was used primarily as a malleable rock rather than as a workable metal. Deposits of iron ore, hematite, were also known. The ore does not appear to have been smelted. Hematite in raw form was worked into fishing net weights for use at one site in Southern Louisiana. It was useful simply as a heavy rock.

Distribution of artifacts among settlements establishes that trade did exist. The known road systems such as Chaco and Hopewell belong to a much later era. If the European model is any indication, it is likely that commerce was riverine in nature. Given the reach of the Mississippi and its tributaries, secondary trade could have extended for more than a thousand miles.

At the time of the Santorini eruption the Native American population had, through the long process of adaptation to varied environments, subdivided itself into many cultures and Stone Age hunter-gatherer units.

The habitation of one such group has been excavated at Poverty Point in Louisiana. The site was active from about 1700 BC until about 1300 BC. During this time there was no visible break in activity that might be attributed to volcanic winter. In fact, the site was similar to an earlier settlement at Watson Brake in the same general area, suggesting that no cultural or economic disruption had occurred for centuries.

That is not to suggest that the volcanic winter caused by the Santorini eruption did not impact America. Dendrochronology clearly indicates that it did. The fact that the impact is not visible in the archaeological record left by the Native Americans of the time suggests that their hunter-gatherer lifestyle insulated them from the effects.

One clue to this can be found in a hunting method called buffalo jumping, used by natives of the plains. In this approach Native American hunters caught herds of bison at their normal watering places and drove a portion of the herd off a nearby cliff. The resulting kill was then harvested for food, clothing, shelter and tools. Estimates of the prehistoric bison population in North America run into the tens of millions. The annual human harvest represented a minuscule percentage of this population. Even a radical thinning of the bison herds by volcanic winter would have left sufficient numbers to sustain the Native American hunters through the crisis.

The concept of America at the time of the Santorini eruption as an isolated land of Stone Age hunter-gatherers has been challenged by some theorists. They are correct in stating that Christopher Columbus was not the first to land in the Americas. Vikings had settled briefly in Newfoundland centuries earlier. The modern Kon Tiki expedition proved that a trans-pacific voyage was possible, although not that one actually happened. Later voyages of discovery established that an Atlantic crossing was possible in appropriately rigged sailing vessels. The crossings were made in vessels sturdily built around a keel and skeleton, not the Bronze Age shipwright's pattern where the hull was the main structural member. The North Atlantic is a particularly fickle mistress. The explorer Sebastian Cabot made the return crossing to Europe in record time one year. The next year his fleet was lost with all hands on the same voyage.

Bronze Age contact with the Old World and the Americas would have brought metal working technology to the Americas. This should have persisted in the Native American cultures that absorbed and adapted it to their own lifestyles. Native Americans were rapid and voracious consumers of advanced technology when it suited their purposes.

Perhaps the best known example from the historical period arises from the engagement of tribes of the Sioux and Northern Cheyenne with the US Seventh Cavalry on Montana's Little Big Horn River in 1876 AD. The engagement has been enshrined in American folklore as Custer's last stand. A brush fire in the late 20th Century AD cleared the battle site of undergrowth, allowing archaeologists to cover the area with metal detectors and develop a comprehensive map of the distribution of artifacts. Of particular interest were cartridge casings from the rifles used. Eyewitness accounts state that the Seventh Cavalry was entirely reliant on firearms; no saber was carried by any member of the command. The Seventh Cavalry carried single shot .45-55 Springfield carbines. All other rifle casings could be attributed to Native American weapons.

When the survey was completed the cartridge casings from Native American weapons were subjected to forensic examination similar to that used in modern criminal investigation. It was determined that Native American forces brought over two hundred cartridge loading repeating rifles to the engagement. This type rifle was a post-civil war development. It had been in existence for only about ten years prior to the engagement. Native Americans had seized on European technology and used it to immediate advantage.

If Native Americans had rapidly adopted European technology in the Nineteenth Century AD, there is no reason to think they wouldn't have done so in the Seventeenth Century BC. The absence of such technology in the development of Native American culture is a strong argument that America was an isolated region at the time of the Santorini eruption. The ancestors of its inhabitants had survived the Younger Dryas calamity. The inhabitants of 1600 BC survived their own volcanic winter.

Isolation and a primitive lifestyle seems to have insulated the Native Americans from much of the impact volcanic winter visited on cultures that had grown reliant on agriculture and commerce. Such was not the case when the stratospheric winds that brought it carried the sulfate aerosol veil eastward across the Atlantic to the cultures of Europe.

A CLOUD OVER EUROPE

At the time of the Santorini eruption the trans-alpine areas of Northern and Central Europe, as well as the British Isles and the Iberian Peninsula, were home to Bronze Age economies rooted in agriculture and animal husbandry. The settlements excavated by archaeologists tend to be village-sized enclaves sited to take advantage of local resources. Mineral resources were exploited where available. Distribution of artifacts across the continent establishes the existence of a wide-spread trade network. The commercial and administrative centers that must have existed to support this network have remained elusive.

Evidence of how some of this trade was carried out comes in the form of an artifact called the *Dover Boat*. The well preserved remains were discovered during excavation for a railroad tunnel under the English Channel between Britain and France. The *Dover Boat* has been dated between 1575 and 1520 BC. Modern occupation above the site prevented complete removal of the boat, but a thirty foot section was cut off and removed for examination. A replica has been made and successfully floated and maneuvered. Safety concerns precluded sea trials, but there is no indication it could not have withstood the rigors of a trip across the Channel.

The English Channel is the narrowest expanse of sea between England and France. As such it is subject to Venturi effect. Winds from the north are squeezed into a progressively narrower passage. In order to move the same volume of air through a restricted space in the same time the air must gain speed. The increase in wind velocity raises high waves. The harrowing six or so hour journey rowing across the Channel in the *Dover Boat* would have required a seasoned professional crew.

Strict point to point navigation was not required. As long as general direction and the topography of the destination shore were known it would have been possible to make the crossing to any point on the opposite shore and follow known landmarks to the desired destination port. Supporting this endeavor would require a trading establishment with permanent port locations and repair and maintenance facilities.

This trading establishment connected England and the mainland at a time when a continental culture called Unetice flourished. Unetice was prevalent in Central Europe. Close to 2,500 sites have been located in the Czech Republic, Slovakia, Poland and Germany. Their ceramic and metal products, normal trade goods of the time, have been excavated in locations from Ireland to Italy to Scandinavia to the Balkans. Unetice arose around 2300 BC and lasted until 1600 BC. At the time of the Santorini eruption they were the influential if not the dominant European culture.

Only a few of the excavated settlements were large, with one containing a long house measuring approximately eighty by twenty feet. The majority of settlements appear to have been village level agricultural establishments. The presence of settlements of differing scale suggests a structured and stratified society. The *Dover Boat* speaks to an organized and professionalized commercial network, rather than a haphazard conglomeration of villages exchanging goods over time-honored paths.

DNA results from Unetice burials show less Yamnaya ancestry than predecessor cultures, suggesting some resurgence of the indigenous population following the Yamnaya influx. The presence of related haplogroups 12, 12a1 and 12c2 indicate that ancestry as well as culture helped define the Unetice. The burials themselves are unique. With few exceptions in the many inhumations that have been excavated, the corpses were aligned North and South, with the head to the South and turned to face east. The purpose of this posing is not known, but it is clear evidence of a uniform belief system. Equally mysterious is the most famous Unetice artifact, the *Nebra Sky Disk*. The *Disk* suggests astronomical sophistication and testifies to the skills of the people who made it, but tells us little of their culture.

The closest thing we have to writing from the Unetice culture is a collection of clay (and occasionally stone) artifacts that are generically named the *Enigmatic Tablets*. These are found both within and beyond the Unetice geography, and may have been used to document trade. They contain markings that are generally geometric, consisting of points, lines and regular shapes. A recent effort to scan and collate the known tablets has yet to produce any decipherment. In the absence of written history, we are left with the question of how and why a complex and successful civilization built up over the course of some seven hundred years vanished fairly abruptly around 1600 BC.

While we have no written account of the aftermath of the Santorini eruption's volcanic winter on Europe in 1600 BC, we do have contemporary records of a comparable eruption in the Nineteenth Century AD. On April 10, 1815 AD Mount Tambora in the East Indies erupted. Greenland ice cores showed a significant spike in sulfates. Contemporary newspaper accounts record the effect in Europe. Superimposing these accounts on cultural and commercial civilizations of the Middle Bronze Age will provide insight into the probable impact of the Santorini eruption.

Nineteenth Century AD accounts of volcanic winter speak of widespread crop failures and significant losses of livestock. Food prices rose dramatically in Germany. Famine gripped Ireland. Rioting, arson and looting swept major European cities. The growing industrial sophistication of Europe in the Nineteenth Century AD was detrimental rather than helpful. Workers in cities and factory towns had to eat, but they produced no food themselves. The Bronze Age technology of 1600 BC would have had the same effect. Europe of 1815/16 AD was at the mercy of climate, as it would have been in 1600 BC when the Santorini eruption brought a comparable volcanic winter.

The impact on Bronze Age Europe would have been worse. Worldwide commerce using money as a medium of exchange was thousands of years in the future. Instead, networks of scattered villages produced the crops and livestock not only to feed the larger commercial settlements, but also to provide excess to be used as trade goods. Without agricultural trade, commerce would wither. Crafts people and merchants who depended on trade would be without a livelihood. The Unetice elite would have found itself in an untenable position. The carefully developed and nurtured economic system that underpinned their culture was subjected to a sudden failure that stretched over their known world. There was no place to turn for help.

Unetice culture did not simply wither and die. It suffered what appears to be an abrupt replacement by a culture called Tumulus, after their custom of burying their elite dead in mounds referred to as tumuli. Unfortunately they left no writing to describe their civilization or the events of their history. Artifacts from the Tumulus burials establish them as a warrior culture. They appear to have expanded from the southern reaches of Unetice culture northward and eastward, and are thought to have established themselves in chiefdoms in the areas they overran. Their larger settlements were strongly fortified, suggesting that either their conquests may have been tenuous or there was internecine competition that regularly turned violent. The larger question is how the Tumulus came to dominate a significant portion of Europe.

Based on recoveries from the incumbent Unetice settlements, the elite and possibly a subordinate warrior class were well armed. Numerous bronze swords and daggers have been found in widely scattered locations, representing state of the art armaments for the time. The Unetice were well prepared to defend their holdings. Given their long history they had almost certainly been compelled to do so in the past. For the Unetice to have fallen abruptly from power after some seven hundred years of successful development and influence provides further evidence of a sudden weakening in their civilization.

The Tumulus culture seems to have seized control of the Unetice commercial and agricultural structure rather than wiping it out. Trade continued throughout the Tumulus dominance, ranging from 1600 to 1200 BC. There are indications, however, that the Tumulus also engaged regularly in banditry and pillage. This could simply be the result of an aggressive mind set. It could also suggest that resources were scarce during the aftermath of volcanic winter. The influx of a new population would have put a strain on the existing agricultural and commercial base.

The details of how the Tumulus gained control are lost to history, but an episode later in the Tumulus dominance may offer some clues. In the Thirteenth Century BC a battle was fought in the Tollense valley of Northern Germany. The prize appears to have been a causeway, probably a choke point on an important trade route. This was not a village level skirmish. Estimates of force size range from 3,000 to 5,000 combatants, with perhaps as many as 1,000 killed.

Raising armies of such magnitude required a high order of military organization and training. Fielding them required a reliable chain of logistics. Using them effectively required strategic planning and complex execution. Exploration of the battlefield made it clear that the level of governance and administration in Europe in the Bronze Age had advanced to a much greater level of sophistication than previously thought.

The dead at Tollense appeared to have been stripped of anything of value and thrown into the river as an expedient means of disposal. Many of the remains presented signs of previous trauma that had healed since it was inflicted. This established that a number of the combatants were experienced and probably professional soldiers. A policy of abandonment of the dead in situ meant that no trace of any large battle ever appeared in archaeological excavations of the graves associated with settlements.

This is certainly the case in modern times. During World War I massed artillery and grazing machine gun fire made the retrieval of hundreds of thousands of remains from the no man's land between the trench lines in Belgium and France impossible. Future archaeologists unfamiliar with the battle locations would not be able to determine the scope or scale of devastation from examination of settlement burials. The same may well have been true in conflicts between the Tumulus and the Unetice centuries earlier, masking the details of the Tumulus take over.

If we do not have direct evidence of a military crisis experienced by the Unetice culture in 1600 BC, then we will need to make what we can of indirect indications. A good place to start is the story of the discovery and analysis of the *Nebra Sky Disk,* the most famous of the surviving Unetice artifacts. The *Disk* is the oldest known portable representation of astronomical objects in the world. Scholarship at the time of discovery was steeped in the tradition of trans-alpine Europe as a land of barbarians. It took patient effort and analysis before the *Disk* was accepted as genuine.

The *Disk* was found along with two bronze swords, two hatchets, a chisel and bracelet fragments by treasure hunters using a metal detector on an illicit foray in the German woods. They damaged the *Disk* in the process of extracting it from its burial place and destroyed part of the site. As looters, and thus subject to prosecution under German law, they sold the hoard as quickly as possible. The hoard made its way through the black market for some time before being intercepted by the police. The artifacts were traced back to the looters. As part of a plea bargain they took the authorities to the site where they had found the hoard. The location was verified when excavation produced a sliver of gold that fit precisely a void in the decoration of the *Disk*.

The site proved to be the remains of a prehistoric enclosed settlement. The relics were dated to between 1600 and 1560 BC by radiocarbon analysis of a piece of birch bark embedded in one of the swords. This, of course, is a date of burial, not of manufacture. Analysis established that both the gold used in the initial phase of construction of the *Disk* and the tin content of the bronze portion originated in Cornwall, in Britain. The *Disk* is either of local manufacture or local modification. Its final form was achieved in four phases. In the second phase gold of a separate origin was used to construct two arcs, whose span was eighty two degrees apart. This is the correct angle between sunset at the summer and winter solstice at fifty one degrees north latitude where the *Disk* was recovered. Additional modifications followed in subsequent years, or perhaps decades.

The purpose of the *Nebra Sky Disk* is still being debated. The two most prominent schools champion either religious or astronomical usage. There is no evidence that the Unetice perceived any difference between religion and astronomy. It is clear that the *Disk* held a position of importance in Unetice culture, and that it had for some time before its burial. The question of why it was taken out of whatever vital service it performed and subsequently buried has only one reasonable answer. It was put away for safekeeping during a period of crisis. In 1600 BC the crisis at hand was the volcanic winter produced by the Santorini eruption and the concurrent Tumulus expansion.

Neither volcanic winter nor the Tumulus expansion was limited to the territory of central Europe dominated by the Unetice. The Tumulus moved eastward into the Carpathian Basin and northward through Poland. Indications of Tumulus culture have been noted as far westward as France. Neither the Unetice nor the Tumulus expanded beyond Continental Europe.

In Britain the Wessex culture had been established since the late third millennium BC. Wessex is associated with later development of the Stonehenge complex on Salisbury Plain. The complex was begun in the Stone Age, around 3100 BC, and was used and expanded by a succession of cultures into the Bronze Age. The Wessex culture is credited with placement of the massive stone monoliths, and with many burials in the area. Around 1600 BC activity on Salisbury Plain ended. To credit the aftermath of the Santorini eruption for this is speculation, but it is noteworthy that a site in constant use and improvement for fifteen hundred years would go dark in the aftermath of volcanic winter.

Wessex culture changed dramatically enough around 1600 BC for scholars to divide it into Wessex I, prior to 1600 BC, and Wessex II thereafter. Most obvious was a change in disposal of the dead. Wessex I practiced inhumation, while Wessex II practiced cremation. Other changes left no fingerprints on history. One thing that did not change was trade. By virtue of geography Wessex II retained control of substantial deposits of tin and gold, as well as other resources. Their need for imported commodities did not vanish. Evidence from the Must Farms excavation established that the trade network extended at least as far as Italy.

Prehistoric Scandinavia, linked mainly by trade to Britain and the rest of Europe, also felt the impact of volcanic winter. Dendrochronology from Sweden establishes a date range contemporaneous with the Santorini eruption, but tells us nothing of the Nordic civilizations that had to deal with the event. We have a wealth of rock carvings from the era. These are pictorial in nature and do not provide any historical narrative. A predominance of boats and battle scenes suggest an aggressive, sea-faring culture prone to conflict. What impact volcanic winter may have had on the conflicts or their outcome cannot be determined from the carvings.

A similar historical vacuum prevails in Southern Europe, particularly in the Iberian Peninsula. DNA suggests this area, along with the Island of Sardinia, did not incur replacement during the Yamnaya migration. The Pyrenees Mountains and the Mediterranean were physical barriers to commingling. Geographic, ancestral and cultural separation from the rest of Europe may have provided some insulation, not from the physical effects of volcanic winter but from migration and cultural incursion that might otherwise have resulted from pressures on neighboring civilizations.

Today's Europe is a land of cultural enclaves, some of whose origins may echo back to the Bronze Age. Without any written narrative or marked change in DNA it is not possible to trace them to the events of 1600 BC.

The truth is that we know very little of prehistoric Europe. Much of our scanty knowledge comes to us by random accident. Had the Spanish railway authority not needed to cut a right of way through a mountainous area we would not have known that the ancestors of modern man occupied Europe more than a million years ago. Other discoveries have come through the fortuitous finds of construction firms, farmers, spelunkers and others. Far more burials than settlements have been uncovered. Given the proclivity of man to build and re-build on the same site, it is possible that civilizations from the Bronze Age lie entombed and unknown beneath modern cities.

The first cohesive written narrative of Europe north of the Alps comes to us in Julius Caesar's First Century BC account of his Gallic Wars. Subsequent Roman writing gives us civilization's view of a barbarian land and culture. As an example, much has been made in modern times of the First Century AD revolt of Britain's Iceni under the leadership of Queen Boudieca. Briefly summarized, Boudieca's forces ambushed a Roman Army column and sacked and burned several Roman coastal towns, including the port of Londinium, before turning inland. The Roman commander, Gaiuis Suetonius, gathered the remainder of Rome's northern garrison and set off in cautious pursuit while he awaited help from the southern garrison. Before Suetonius' reinforcements arrived, the barbarians turned and attacked the badly outnumbered Romans. The battle was an epic disaster for the Iceni. They had no experience fighting a head-to-head engagement against a professional army. The barbarian survivors quit the field in disarray. Boudieca remains as a footnote to history courtesy of two pages in Tacitus' voluminous *Annals of Imperial Rome.* No British record survives, if indeed any was ever set down.

We can infer from the narrative that a fairly sophisticated road network must have existed, based on the size of armies involved in the movement. Prehistoric roads are known to underline portions of the modern British motorway system. Scholars have not found the site of the decisive battle described by Tacitus, and have only a vague notion of where it might have occurred. Our limited knowledge of an event in the fairly well documented Roman era illustrates the difficulty of drawing conclusions about happenings more than sixteen centuries earlier.

The occupants of Europe at the time may well have heard the Santorini eruption. The lesser 1883 AD eruption that split the Pacific island of Krakatoa was heard 3,600 miles away in Australia. Unlike the Greeks, whose impressions survive in later dramatic works, the trans-alpine Europeans left no lore that was later recorded for posterity. The trans-alpine Europeans also would not have known that volcanic winter was approaching from the opposite direction.

We do not have enough information to assess the full impact of that winter on Europe. There are indications of profound cultural shifts. Whether consequences of those shifts have filtered down to the political organization we know today we can only surmise. At most they would represent only a minuscule fraction of the worldwide legacy of the Santorini eruption.

THE LEGACY

The legacy of Atlantis began in the subterranean depths, beyond the sight and certainly beyond the control of humankind. The endless, imperceptible creep of tectonic plates fueled a cycle that built enormous pressure in the fissures of the earth. Pressure that eventually vented in a series of eruptions in 1600 BC, shattering the island of Santorini, blasting part of it into the sky and sloughing huge masses of earth into the sea. Residents of the Island, warned by the rumblings and ventings of coming catastrophe, made good their escape from the immediate danger. Escape from the effects of the resulting tsunami and the volcanic winter that followed was not possible. The eruption's aftermath would involve and irrevocably change much of the civilized world.

By 1600 BC large portions of the humankind had found their way into the Bronze Age. The primitive survival skills of hunting and gathering had long since been replaced by the more efficient techniques of agriculture and animal husbandry. Social organization grew more complex as portions of the population were able to specialize in crafts and engage in commerce. Cities and seaports grew to support long range trade. Pastoral chiefdoms were consolidated into kingdoms. Royal capitols became centers of administration and learning, technology and culture.

Progress did not come without consequences. Populations expanded in the confines of a finite world. Competition for scarce resources sharpened.

Professional armies grew out of the need for protection and royal ambition. Disputes that could not be resolved by commercial negotiation or diplomatic art were settled at spear point. Hostile kingdoms existed in a precarious balance of power. A balance that fell victim to events growing out of the Santorini eruption.

Beyond the Santorini itself, the most immediate and direct victim of the eruption was the Eastern Mediterranean maritime trade network. The massive tsunami created by the eruption obliterated seaports on the main Minoan island of Crete. It did sufficient damage to ports on the coast of Egypt to bring a halt to northbound sailings from that country. The eastern coast of mainland Greece, in particular the Saronic Gulf in the southeast, facing Santorini, was hit with tidal force catastrophic enough to merit being memorialized in the drama of a later period. Legends of great waves can be found in the folklore of ancient civilizations living along the Eastern Mediterranean coasts.

Loss of Eastern Mediterranean maritime trade would have repercussions for much of the commercially interconnected world of the time, but the worst was still on the horizon. Sulfate compounds blown into the stratosphere by the eruption were carried around the globe by powerful upper level winds. Unlike the visible ash that settled out fairly quickly, these compounds existed in aerosol form. They persisted over months, if not years, reflecting the incoming energy of the sun away from the Earth and producing volcanic winter.

For the people in its path, volcanic winter was suffocating. Crops withered and failed. Domestic animals died for lack of graze. With the failure of agriculture and animal husbandry crafts people and merchants who traded their wares for the necessities of life found themselves without a market. Many caught in the grip of famine and destitution must have wondered whether the gods they had worshipped long and faithfully had deserted them. As economies faltered, the political and social structures they supported weakened. Existing balances of power deteriorated and new players rose.

In the wake of the catastrophe the Egyptians were able to expel the Hyksos and emerge as an imperial power. The Hittites, through a combination of conquest and spear-point diplomacy, seized control of a good part of what is now Syria and Turkey. The Mycenaeans went from being the hired mercenaries of the Minoans to their hosts and eventual overlords. They consolidated the city-states of mainland Greece and the nearby islands into a third empire. The overall outcome was unstable and unsustainable. Internal and external pressures, exacerbated by mutual conflict over limited available lands, eventually destroyed the three empires.

Farther afield the city of Babylon, whose power had been waning, found new life under the Kassites. West Eurasians fled with their gods and their culture and established themselves as rulers of the Indian subcontinent. In China the Shang Dynasty exploited volcanic winter as heaven's mandate for change. Their rise began the process of urbanization and conquest that would one day result in the consolidation of the vast geographic area of China under a single national flag.

That upheaval was rampant in the aftermath of the Santorini eruption is undeniable. It is fair to ask what difference the turmoil could possibly make thirty six centuries after the ash settled.

To begin to answer the question, we need look no farther than the page on which it is printed. This book is written in alphabetic style characters. The character set, consisting of twenty six units, is capable of producing a large combination of words that require no pictorial supplement and can represent any spoken syllable.

Alphabetic writing appears to have evolved from a combination of hieratic and hieroglyphic Egyptian. The earliest examples of the script, dating from about 1800 BC, were discovered at a turquoise mine on the Sinai Peninsula. Many of the miners were Canaanite. Later examples began turning up in Canaan. The Egyptians controlled Canaan during most of the New Kingdom. It is likely that the script migrated northward during this period.

The language of commerce and diplomacy during the Eastern Mediterranean imperial period was Akkadian, rendered in complex cuneiform. In the period following the Santorini eruption, the use of Akkadian was enforced by Egyptian and Hittite control. When the Hittite Empire crumbled and Egypt withdrew from Canaan, newly liberated city-states along the Eastern Mediterranean coast were free to use whatever language and form of writing they found convenient. Prominent among the emerging cultures were the Phoenicians. They were largely responsible for the export of the alphabet we use today. The earliest example dates to about 1050 BC.

Progression from pictographic to syllabic to alphabetic writing is not natural. The Egyptians continued to use hieroglyphics for another fifteen centuries. East Asian pictorial writing continues to this day. It was the rise of Egypt in the wake of the Santorini eruption that allowed the migration of alphabetic script north along the Eastern Mediterranean coast. The subsequent failure of the Egyptian and Hittite Empires, itself a consequence of forces set in place by the aftermath of the eruption, released alphabetic script to be spread broadcast by the Phoenicians.

A second legacy of the Santorini eruption is less clearly defined. When we look at modern mathematics we think in terms of a base ten numbering system derived from the number of fingers on human hands, and rules of geometry formulated by Greek thinkers beginning sometime before 600 BC. On closer examination, the situation isn't that simple. The hours, minutes and seconds by which we reckon time are set according to a base sixty numbering system. The Greeks saw mathematics as originating in Egypt.

Egyptian mathematics, essential to support large construction projects and annual re-survey following the Nile floods, appears to be more practical than rigorous. For example, the Egyptians did not have a concept of Pi (the ratio between the circumference and diameter of a circle). They would approximate the area of a circle of a diameter of nine units by the area of a square eight units on a side. This square has an area (8 X 8) equal to 64. Using the correct formula for the area of a circle, multiplying Pi by the square of the radius, (3.14159 X 9/2 X 9/2) returns a result of 63.617, an imprecision of less than one percent. While this may sound crude, modern computers use the same strategy. Rather than store numbers for Pi or trigonometric functions, they approximate them by iterating the appropriate infinite series until the difference between the derived value and the actual value is too small to make any practical difference.

Babylonian mathematics is the source of the base sixty numbering systems currently in use. Compared to the Egyptian system, Babylonian mathematics was considerably advanced. Their approach to algebra allowed them to solve quadratic and cubic equations. One contemporary source, usually cited as *Tablet Plimpton 322,* hints at some expertise in trigonometry. As with the Egyptians, most of the surviving contemporary material is in the form of tables and solved problems. We have some insight into what they knew, but not the reasoning process by which they came to know it.

The larger question for our examination is how similarities between ancient mathematics and modern practice relate to the Santorini eruption. It is clear from inspection that the lines of reasoning that led to the Egyptian and Babylonian systems of mathematics must have been very different. Although the two systems existed at the same time, they were worlds apart in terms of the geography and the cultures in which they functioned. It is unusual that both would contribute components to modern mathematics.

The route taken by the Egyptian system is the clearer of the two. Any student who has suffered through Euclidian geometry can testify to the Greek contribution. The Greeks, specifically Herodotus and Aristotle, credit the Egyptians with the beginnings of their mathematical reasoning. It was the Santorini eruption that brought both the Egyptians and the Mycenaeans to imperial status and opened regular commerce and communication between Egypt and the land that would become Greece.

The path taken by Babylonian mathematics also runs through Greece. Pioneering mathematicians of the Sixth Century BC, Thales and Pythagoras, journeyed to Babylon to study. Tradition has Thales returning to the Greek sphere and predicting the solar eclipse of 585 BC.

The survival of Babylonian mathematics from the Eighteenth Century BC of Hammurabi to the Sixth Century BC of Nebuchadnezzar was tied to the survival of Babylon as a cosmopolitan center. The city was nearing the end of a downward trend at the time of the Santorini eruption. The resulting volcanic winter sent the Hittites eastward looking for plunder to sustain themselves. Their sack of Babylon cleared the way for a takeover by the Kassites, who enshrined the city as their administrative center for the succeeding four hundred years. Once established, Babylon remained prominent for centuries to follow, allowing the Babylonian system of reckoning to outlive the city where it was born.

The legacies of alphabetic writing and mathematics are benign. A contentious inheritance grew out of the collapse of the Mycenaean Empire; democracy as we know it today. The word is a combination of two Greek words, demos, meaning people and kratos, meaning rule.

The foundations were laid when the Santorini eruption sent Minoans fleeing to the sanctuary of mainland Greece, held at the time by the warlords who provided mercenaries to secure Minoan maritime commerce. The Minoan model of distributed governance fit neatly with the existing Mycenaean confederation of city-states. City-states maintained much of their autonomy, rather than being absorbed into a centrally controlled kingdom. In time the Empire failed, both militarily abroad and politically at home. The ingrained culture of autonomous city-states remained.

When the Achaean raiders of Troy had faded into legend, the populations of the cities they left behind began to take charge of their own destiny. It was the beginning of a long and not always successful battle against tyranny. Had the Santorini eruption not driven Minoan wealth, power and civilization into Greece, the city-state governance model might never have taken root. Had the aftermath of the eruption not sown the seeds of the destruction of the Mycenaean Empire, the rise of an independent-minded citizenry might never have happened.

Historians like to credit the growth of democracy to the people whose ideas and actions shaped it. That is certainly valid, but there can be no growth without fertile ground to support it. If talk of democracy had flared up in a centralized tyranny, it would have been crushed immediately under the sandals of a professional army. Only in the autonomous cities such as those of classical Greece could it have lasted long enough to take root. They were the outgrowth of a process set in place by the Santorini eruption.

The Indian subcontinent saw a polar opposite to the legacy of democracy. Volcanic winter drove a migration from Eurasia across the Spin Gar Mountains into the north of the subcontinent. The migrants, through a combination of conquest in the north and infiltration into the south, brought Hindu religion, strict social stratification and Indo-European language. The outcome persists, albeit with some modification, to this day. The gods of the Hindu pantheon are still worshipped. Although the tyranny of the caste system has been broken by law, the system remains largely intact. The Old Sanskrit language has faded into history but its impact remains in both modern language and in the old Vedas it conveyed.

It is not surprising that modern cultural sensitivities offer some rebellion against these notions. People of Indian descent look at the DNA evidence and classify it as Ancient North Indian and Ancient South Indian, rather than seeing migrants from Eurasia and an incumbent population. The term Aryan, with its modern connotations, also makes the notion of a Eurasian legacy from the Santorini eruption distasteful. Recent British occupation of the subcontinent stirs further resentment. Looking back in history, the people of India see their ancestors as urbane and civilized when the people of Britain painted themselves blue and worshipped trees.

Stripped of modern cultural interpretations, the Indian subcontinent is a melting pot that has fused together the contributions of native populations, immigrants from east and west as well as invaders from Macedonia, Afghanistan and Britain. Migration in the aftermath of the Santorini eruption was an important step in the process, and deserves to be recognized for the legacy it left behind.

In China volcanic winter came at a pivotal point in the history of a developing land. The rural agriculture that had developed along the two great rivers, the Yellow and the Yangtze, had grown to the point that it could support more than a simple village society. The Bronze Age had arrived, and with it the need for commerce and crafts to fully exploit the new technology. The Erlitou Culture began the transformation to centralized social organization on a larger scale. A shift from rule by popular acclamation to inheritance by birth right brought the Xia Dynasty to power.

The Xia Dynasty fell to the Shang Dynasty. In 1996 AD a chronological study by the current Chinese Government established that the break in dynasties occurred in 1600 BC. The available clues indicate that the procuring cause of the Shang takeover was the onset of volcanic winter caused by the Santorini eruption. Natural calamity had both physical and spiritual meaning to the Chinese. Hardship demanded action. Calamity signaled that the heavens no longer favored the ruling power.

The Shang brought urbanization to China. They expanded their rule far beyond the limited holdings of the Xia. The Erlitou Culture of the Xia Dynasty is now seen by historians as the transition from rural to urban control. The Shang Dynasty is seen as the beginning of the consolidation and growth of modern China.

By modern standards the expanded holdings of the Shang Dynasty were modest. China would not reach its zenith as a seat of imperial power until the Thirteenth Century AD rule of Kublai Khan, whose control extended from the Pacific Ocean to the Black Sea. The process began with the Shang Dynasty. The Shang Dynasty began with the volcanic winter that followed the Santorini eruption. Volcanic winter was not, by itself, enough to bring about change, but its occurrence at a pivotal point in Chinese history provided the impetus for action.

Volcanic winter struck Europe and America no less harshly, but left no persuasive evidence of a legacy that persists to modern times. The state of evidence is constantly evolving. Legend has the city of Rome, and by extension the Roman Empire, being founded by a fugitive Trojan prince named Aeneas following the destruction of his own city. In modern times the narrative, Virgil's *Aeneid,* has served mainly a source of phrases to torment students of Latin who were struggling to master the mechanics of translation. Recent DNA studies placed some northern Italian ancestry in Anatolia, not far from the site of Troy.

Our insight into the legacy of Atlantis is far from complete. It has necessarily been pieced together from the limited relics and writings that have survived thirty six centuries. It ranges from science to speculation, and leaves much to be learned.

Little doubt remains that the Santorini eruption is the event underlying Plato's dialogues dramatizing the legend of Atlantis. The nature and force of the four phase eruption is reasonably well understood. The behavior of tsunamis and volcanic winter has been reported in recent recorded history. The date of the eruption can be set circa 1600 BC, based on radiocarbon and dendrochronology findings. DNA analysis provides scientifically verifiable insight into the origins and movements of the populations that bore the brunt of the aftermath.

Some of the impact of the eruption and its aftermath can be confidently inferred from writings from the Egyptian and Hittite Empires. More can be reasonably deduced from the cuneiform of Mesopotamia and the Hindu Vedas. Judeo-Christian scripture and the dragon bones of China add additional clues. Corroboration of some dates is available from radiocarbon analysis and astronomical anchoring.

The idea that the founding of Rome can be traced to the fall of Troy is at the far reaches of speculation. Herodotus made note of the story. Many ancient Romans believed it. Julius Caesar visited the ruins of Troy. To suggest that modern scholars are skeptical would be an understatement. The line of descent is through a culture called the Etruscans, or Ransa in their parlance, which first appeared in Italy around 1100 BC. Scholars are divided over the role of the Etruscans, if any, in the founding of Rome. The Etruscans were literate. Their earliest known writing dates to around 700 BC. Their language is not well understood. No historical narrative has been gleaned from the thirteen thousand or so examples recovered to date.

The largest missing piece in the tale of Atlantis is the voice of the Minoans. They witnessed the eruption and the physical damage of the immediate aftermath. They knew what part they played in the subsequent rise of the Mycenaean Empire. They were in commercial contact with all the players in the Eastern Mediterranean. Their narrative awaits the decipherment of Linear A.

Identifying smaller pieces of the puzzle will be challenging. Relics and writing may lie unappreciated in academic storage because no one has connected them with Santorini or its aftermath. Tomorrow's archaeological finds, translations and laboratory analyses may suffer the same fate. If we are to understand the legacy of Atlantis, we will need to evaluate what we know today and what we learn tomorrow in the context of the Santorini eruption of 1600 BC.

ADDITIONAL READING

Collapsing the global impact of the Santorini eruption into a digestible narrative is an exercise in summarization. Explanation of the underlying science and archaeological methodology is reduced to the minimum necessary to follow the flow of events. Only those discoveries and translations relative to the story are touched on. No more than minimal space can be allotted to the cultures involved, or to the people who made them up. For those interested in gaining a deeper insight, the following readings are suggested.

Boyer, Carl B. 1968. A History of Mathematics. John Wiley and Sons.

Breasted, James Henry. 1903. *A History of Egypt.* Charles Scribner's Sons.

Castleden, Rodney. 1992. *Minoans: Life in Bronze Age Crete.* Routledge.

Ceram, C. W. (Kurt Merak). 1955. *The Secret of the Hittites.* Alfred A. Knopf.

de Selincourt, Aubrey, 1972, *Translation of Herodotus: The Histories,* Penguin

Evans, Arthur, 1936, *The Palace of Minos at Knossos,* (4 volumes Pub. 1921-1936), MacMillan.

Fagles, Robert. 1998. *Translation of Homer's Iliad.* Penguin Publishing Group.

Fagles, Robert. 1997. *Translation of Homer's Odyssey.* Penguin Publishing Group.

Gardner, Alan. 1905. *The Admonitions of an Egyptian Sage.* Georg Olms Hildesheim.

Jamison, Stephanie W. and Brereton, Joel P. 2014. *Translation of The Rig Veda.* Oxford University Press

Jeans, James. 1947. The Growth of Physical Science. Cambridge University Press.

Jones, Martin. 2001. *Unlocking the Past.* Penguin.

Lee, Sir Duncan. 1977. *Translation of Plato: Timaeus and Critias.* Penguin.

Leick, Gwendolyn. 2001. *Mesopotamia.* Penguin.

MacQueen, J.G. 1986. *The Hittites and their Contemporaries in Asia Minor.* Thames and Hudson.

Olson, Steve. 2016. *Eruption: The Untold Story of Mount St. Helens.* W.W.Norton.

Pope, Maurice. 1999. *The Story of Decipherment.* Thames and Hudson.

Price, T. Douglas. 2013. *Europe Before Rome.* Oxford University Press.

Reich, David. 2018. *Who We Are And How We Got Here, Ancient DNA And The New Science Of The Human Past.* Vintage.

Roberts, J.A.G. 1999. *A Concise History of China.* McGraw Hill

Saggs, H.W.F. 1995. *Babylonians.* The British Museum Press.

Schofield, Louise. 2007. *The Mycenaeans.* The British Museum Press.

Spalinger, Anthony J. 2005. *War in Ancient Egypt.* Blackwell Publishing.

Thomas, David Hurst. 2000. *Exploring Native North America.* Oxford University Press.

Whiston, William. 1999. *Translation: The New Complete Works of Josephus.* Kregel Publications.

Wooley, C. Leonard. 1965. *The Sumerians.* Oxford University Press.

Made in the USA
Las Vegas, NV
05 October 2021